UPON THIS ROCK

UPON THIS ROCK

ERIC W. GOSDEN

Foreword by
NORMAN P. GRUBB

LUTTERWORTH PRESS
Cambridge

Lutterworth Press
7 All Saints' Passage
Cambridge CB2 3LS

British Library Cataloguing in Publication Data
Gosden, Eric W.
  Upon this rock: the sacrifices of a Japanese nurse for a young church.
  1. Converts
  2. Christianity—Japan
  I. Title
  248.2'46   BR1305

  ISBN 0-7188-2684-1

First published 1957
Reprinted by Lutterworth Press 1987

Printed in Great Britain by
The Guernsey Press Co. Ltd., Guernsey, Channel Islands

FOREWORD

THE beauty of Jesus shines out of this Japanese story in a purely Japanese setting, and irradiates the spirit of the reader. Though written by a "foreign missionary", only Jesus and the Japanese are seen. We walk again in the ever-old, ever-new tracks of the Shepherd who finds His other sheep, as He found us, and our hearts sing the song of the angels. Here in the heart of dark Japan, where false gods and lying faiths hold almost universal sway, we thrill to read of the old, old story of grace abounding—the agony of a destitute soul, the change that Jesus makes, the courage, the tenacity, the boldness, the grace, the patience of the Spirit in a weak, human vessel, the 'much fruit' in an intensely conservative Buddhist village, the church built literally at night, the life of self-denial among many adversaries, the glory of the home-going. No redeemed child of God can read this narrative without a glow in its soul: deep calls unto deep.

Eric Gosden has a remarkable facility in making us live with the Japanese for the few hours of our reading. Nothing foreign intrudes—we see, feel, think Japanese. Here we meet the Christ of the Japanese Road. Eric Gosden himself has lived in Japan many years, first arriving there in 1933, and most evidently sits where they sit. He is a senior member of a greatly used band of missionaries who have ministered Christ to the Japanese—the Japan Evangelistic Band. On a recent visit to Japan, several senior Japanese Christians told me that no work of God in Japan had gone deeper than that which the Spirit had wrought through the two founders of the J.E.B., the much loved Barclay F. Buxton and Paget Wilkes. What God did by them can be read in the biography of Barclay Buxton written by his son, Godfrey Buxton, now chairman of the J.E.B., called *The Reward of Faith*; and in the well-known masterpiece on missionary soul-winning by Paget Wilkes, recently republished, *The Dynamic of Service*. Older lovers of Japan can doubtless remember Paget Wilkes' first book which opened the eyes of many of a past generation to the power of the Gospel in Japanese lives, *Missionary Joys in Japan.*

The keynote of the work of the J.E.B. has ever been Christ's *full* salvation, with the emphasis on the 'full'. The Band members have ever sought to dig deep in lives, to lay strong foundations in the new birth, to build an equally strong superstructure on the standard of I Thessalonians 5: 23, "the very God of peace sanctify you wholly"; and God has mightily and outstandingly borne witness to their ministry. Indeed, it has been a testimony not only throughout Japan, but far beyond to the Christian Church in general, of a Saviour who both justifies and sanctifies. Yet what is even more significant, and the hallmark of true missionary service, the humble, radiant, undaunted little Japanese woman of this story is not a child, but a grandchild of the missionary. No missionary is mentioned in the book! It was a Japanese saint who first bore witness to her, a Japanese pastor who nurtured her in Christ, a Japanese evangelist who reaped where she had sown, a Japanese church that was born out of heathendom. A mission fulfilling its destiny.

NORMAN P. GRUBB

CONTENTS

PART I

THE QUARRY OF LIFE

PART II

THE HAND OF THE MASON

PART III

LIVING STONES

8 CONTENTS

PART I

THE QUARRY OF LIFE

"Look unto the rock whence ye were hewn, and to the hole of the pit whence ye were digged."
(Isaiah 51 : 1)

Chapter 1

AN INDELIBLE SCAR

THE rain which had been falling steadily for some hours was changing to a cold, miserable sleet as Takagi San made his way up the long steep hill into Funo village. It was at any time quite a distance from the railhead, and having missed the last bus he was forced to walk through the winter rain. Quite possibly it would be snow by the morning, the first of the season.

As he reached the first houses of the scattered village a figure came down the road towards him. One of the villagers evidently, judging by the wide straw hat and woven straw cape which he wore. There was a single light burning just where they passed, and Takagi San recognised one of his near neighbours. But he passed by with nothing more than a mumbled greeting. Why should he say more, why appear friendly? Who would want to be friends with a jail-bird? And Takagi had only recently completed six months in the county jail. Not that it was altogether his fault.

His business had been the making of wooden pipes for water systems, and perhaps he had been unwise in laying in so big a store of material. Still, how could he have foreseen the advent of cement pipes, stronger and cheaper than those he manufactured? His business had failed and he had had to declare himself bankrupt. Then it was that his creditors had come down upon him and demanded their pound of flesh. They took it, and Takagi went to jail. It had been hard enough for his wife and the four children to eke out an existence while he was away. The rice had often to be watered into gruel, and the wild herbs of the countryside were all they had to give it a little flavour. But they had managed through, and Sumi had been grand. Yes, the oldest girl was a treasure, so smart, reliable, and with her wits about her. She would go far in life.

He was past the first group of houses. Just another fifty yards or so and he would be home. Someone else coming? Yes, a woman this time, walking on high clogs to avoid the mud, and with her paper umbrella half down as she pressed through the driving sleet. Another muttered greeting, yet she had been a close friend of his wife. He had been right in his decision that day. He would get out of the village, for a while at any rate, and hope that when he had paid his debts the people would again respect him. It was well that he had signed up to go to the coal-mines in Yamaguchi, and Sumi should go with him too. She would do well there.

Ah, home at last! He bent low to enter the little wicket gate, the main door having been pulled over to keep out the storm.

"I'm just back."

"Ah, father! Honourably return! How wet you are, you must be soaked to the skin."

"Yes, Sumi, pretty wet, but glad to be home. Where's mother?"

"Just putting baby to sleep. She'll be right here. Here she is now."

"Ah, honourably return, father. We wondered if you would come tonight as you were not on the last bus."

"I just missed it, but I had to come to give you my news."

"What is it, father?" asked Sumi right away.

"No, have your supper first, and then tell us. You must be so tired and hungry," advised honourable mother.

Takagi hung his dripping garments on a nail in the porch, kicked off his rubber boots and went up into the living-room of his house. Soon, changed into his padded kimono, he was eating his simple meal in the warmth of his own family. He was quickly finished and put down his chopsticks with a satisfied grunt.

"Ah, I was certainly hungry. That tasted good!"

"Now, honourable father, what is your news?" demanded Sumi.

"We're going to Yamaguchi to the coal-mines, just you and I, Sumi."

"To the coal-mines?" mother and daughter cried with one voice.

"Yes, but only I will work in the mines. You will keep house for me, Sumi. You see, since our business went to pieces and I had to leave the village for a while, we have been really hard up for money. So I thought that if I went away and worked I could earn a living for us all and keep the home going here.

Mother is needed here to look after the children and our small fields, so you will come with me to shop and cook. It will only be for the winter months when nothing is doing here, and when the cherry blossom blooms we will return. Besides . . . " and he paused.

"Besides what, honourable father?" asked Sumi.

"Oh nothing, I was just thinking of something else. You'll like it, Sumi, coming with me?" He turned her question aside with one of his own.

"Why, yes; but I don't think I can manage very well."

"Oh yes you will, and in any case you must learn to keep house sometime."

It was later that evening when they were alone that Takagi and his wife spoke about the increasing ostracism in the village, which was his other reason for leaving temporarily.

"I'm afraid it leaves you with the heavy end of the burden, mother, but as we pay our debts the villagers will again respect us."

"I don't mind being alone, and we see little of our neighbours during the deep snow of winter. I shall keep busy too making straw sandals and charcoal bales, and in no time you will be back. The only thing is I shall miss bright little Sumi, but you will take good care of her?"

"Not a doubt! She is very able for her years and will benefit by the experience," concluded father.

So it was decided; and in a few days a large bundle of padded quilts was sent ahead, to be followed later by Takagi San and his daughter Sumi-chan. The journey was a new experience to the girl, for she had never been farther than the nearest big town on the occasion of a school excursion. Now they travelled by bus to the railhead, thence down the branch line to Hiroshima, and from there still farther west until they were nearly at the end of Japan's main island.

.   .   .   .   .

Whatever the country, for some reason or other coal-mining areas are always sordid. It seems as if the dirt and grime associated with the extraction from the earth of the shining black diamonds besmirch the countryside and eat into the very soul of the people. Or is it that the already greedy hearts of the mine-owners manifest themselves in the shoddy buildings and the crowded conditions under which they expect the workers to live? Times are changing and a higher conception of the value of human life and personality is becoming common, but when Sumi San reached her destination things were depressing in the extreme.

There was the mine shaft, and around it the necessary engine rooms and company offices, while on the outer circle, crowded and huddled together, were the workers' houses, if such they might be called. It was wet and a dank dark cloud of smoke and steam seemed to overhang the whole community. Her heart sank within her. This was so different from her mountain home with the tree-covered slopes and the clear, rushing streams. How could she exist here? But, stay, father was with her, and it was to help the family back on to its feet that she was there. She would be brave and happy and battle through.

"Is this the place, honourable father?"

"Yes, Sumi. Not a very nice place, but it looks better when the sun is shining."

"I'm sure I'll be happy here, father, with you, and we shall work hard to help honourable mother and the children back home."

"That's right, let's stick it out to the end. Now, we will go first to the company office and find out what accommodation they have for us."

The accommodation was of the poorest, just two rooms on the ground floor of a ramshackle house which they shared with another family. The kitchen was a communal affair. However, it was to be their home and Sumi-chan busied herself with making it so. It was a long day for her from the time her father left early in the morning until he returned at night; but the time they spent together in the evening was the highlight of the day, while an outing on the occasional holiday the company granted was a rare treat. At fifteen Sumi-chan should just have been completing her school work, but family affairs had made it necessary for her to leave early. So some of the hours in Yamaguchi were filled with study. Best of all, money was coming in and helping to pay off the debts back home.

Some weeks had passed when, coming home one evening, her father said:

"A new young fellow is working along with me these days, but he's fed up with his lodgings. How about letting one of our rooms to him? We could do with the extra cash, and he seems to be a nice fellow."

"Well, honourable father, whatever you say; but I like it with just ourselves here, and the place is not very big to take in another one."

"That's so, but we only have another couple of months here, and we could put up with the inconvenience. He would have his meals with us, and cooking for three is much the same as cooking for two."

"All right, honourable father, if you feel it is right, and if he is a reliable fellow."

So it was that Shigeru San came into the house next day. He was a lad of less than twenty years whose home was at a distance, but who, like Takagi San, was making his living at the mines. He was quiet, almost surly, and did not go out and about much like many of the young fellows in the town. Yet sometimes, when she lifted her eyes from her books or her sewing, Sumi-chan saw him gazing at her with a strange smile on his face. But she thought little of it at the time, taking it to be one of his mannerisms.

It was just a matter of days before Takagi and his daughter were due to return home. Shigeru San had a day off from the mines and had hung about the house most of the day. In the afternoon he came into the room where Sumi-chan was studying and said:

"Sumi-chan, you're going home soon, eh?"

"Yes, and I'm so glad to get away from this smoky place, back to the green mountains of my native place."

"Sumi-chan, I wish you weren't going!"

"Do you?"

"Yes, I have come to like you these days, and would like to have you near me always. Look, I have a suggestion."

Shigeru was speaking fast and excitedly now.

"Your father is out. Let us get some things together and go off somewhere. I have saved up some money and we can enjoy ourselves. I can make you happy. I can give you a good time. And I will work hard when we get elsewhere and will look after you. I will. . . ."

"Shigeru San, I could never, never do that. You may like me, but I could never like you in that way. Besides, I have to help my mother and father get the business back on to its feet and pay our debts. Please go out of this room, and please, please never mention this matter to me again. I could never do such a thing."

The boy was greatly excited now, intent upon carrying into effect the thing he had so often conjured up in his fancy. Sumi-chan was helpless to resist, and though she cried out no one heard and she was soon silenced.

A few days later Takagi and Sumi-chan returned to their mountain home. What a warm welcome awaited them, but Sumi seemed strangely quiet. The bright life of helping her father and mother so unselfishly seemed to be overshadowed. A cloud covered her soul, she felt like a criminal carrying her awful secret locked up in her heart and dreading discovery. It would have been good if she had told her parents of her terrible experience, but she kept it to herself. And the bright girl just out of school developed gradually into a young woman suspicious of the intentions of others.

The cherry blossoms bloomed in their unsullied beauty and fell at their peak in ten thousand petals. But Sumi San could only reflect that at the start of her life her purity had been sullied by one stronger than she was; a purity she could never regain.

Chapter 2

FORMED UNDER PRESSURE

WITH the coming of spring in Japan the winter days of inactivity are over for the mountain farmers. There is the year's supply of wood to be cut from the mountainside, bundled up and carried out from the forest and taken home. The wheat has to be hoed and weeded, the rape-seed carefully tended to ensure a good supply of seed-oil for the family. With lengthening days comes increasing work, and Sumi was glad to busy herself with farm life. It helped her to forget her trouble, and besides it was her duty to help the family.

A little ray of light and cheer came into her life. This was Kazuo San, a boy she had known at school. In her village, as in every other in Japan, the boys and girls find their interests among those of their own sex. It is highly "modern" to walk out with a young man and frowned upon as being in poor taste. But she saw him occasionally, as, for example, when a group of villagers went up to a nearby pass to view the cherry blossoms. The good-natured chit-chat and happy laughter did Sumi good. Life was not too bad after all—especially if Kazuo San was around. They contrived a little conversation together, and the affection between them was mutual. Any community project brought them together, and the building of a washed-out footbridge, or the cleaning out of irrigation ditches, in which all the villagers joined, were occasions eagerly anticipated.

At the same time as the wheat ripened, the silkworms were hatched out of their eggs. Then it was day-and-night work, especially just before the worms went up into their cocoons. Silkworms are voracious eaters, and mulberry leaves had to be plucked in great quantities from the fields. Sumi San and her mother were heavy-eyed from lack of sleep and from constantly attending the worms. But at last the cocoons were made, gathered up and sold through the Farmers' Co-operative.

Now the wheat was ready to harvest. Then the rice seedlings

had to be planted out and cared for by constant weeding. But with the end of the rainy season and the coming of the hot "dog days" the farmers were able to ease up a little. With August came the O Bon Festival, and with it another opportunity to see Kazuo, even at a distance. O Bon was a happy time; and though the villagers believed that the spirits of the departed came back at that time, it was more than anything a time for eating, drinking and revelry. The gods at best were but summarily worshipped.

It was towards the end of the year, and the farmers' cycle of work had nearly completed the full round, when one day it was suggested to Sumi San that she should go to Kobe.

"There's been a man in the village lately recruiting girls to work at a spinning mill in Kobe. The girls live in the dormitory on the compound, have all their food provided, and get good wages into the bargain. How about your going, Sumi?"

In a moment there flashed across her mind the terrible end of her last journey "abroad", and her suspicions of the world and of the glib men who people it. But there could be no danger there, surely. She would be in the security of the dormitory with other girls, with whom she could spend her free time. Besides, the money she sent home would greatly help the family during the dead, profitless months of winter.

"I don't think I want to go, honourable father. Couldn't I stay here and do some work in the house during the winter?"

"There's not the work to do in this mountain village. Our fields are so small, and the growing season so short, that the place just stinks of poverty. It would help us no end in the family here, and you would get home for New Year and the O Bon Festival. The men said something too about the girls going to High School. You'd like to get in some more study, wouldn't you, Sumi?"

"Why, yes, honourable father; if there's the opportunity for High School work perhaps I ought to go."

"Right! We'll see the man tomorrow and try to get fixed up."

No sooner said than done, and before very long Sumi San had moved down to Kobe.

Life in the factory dormitory was a new experience for Sumi San, but she soon fitted in. There were six girls in her room, one of them mothering the rest. Her day was regulated by the mill authorities, almost geared to the spinning machines that rattled in the factory most of the twenty-four hours of each day. Throughout the hours of her shift she worked the four machines allotted to her, and when the evening came she was off to High School. Life was full and she was too busy to think much about the problems that had confused her. So she passed her seventeenth birthday, and was happy in the knowledge her little monthly remittance helped the folk back home.

One night, returning from school somewhat earlier than usual, she passed a little group of people standing on a street corner. Some of them held lanterns, another a drum, while one was standing in the centre of the ring speaking. She stopped with her friends to listen. The group could hardly be called attractive, but she was impressed by their earnestness and obvious sincerity.

"Who are they?" she asked a companion.

"They are followers of Christianity. Can't you see the red cross on the laterns?"

"Oh that! I thought that was something to do with the Red Cross Society, a hospital or something."

The others laughed at her and said, "Well, Sumi San, you are a real country bumpkin. Haven't you heard of Christianity?"

"No! We have one Tenrikyo house in our village, but all the rest only worship Buddha. What are they saying? Let's listen a while."

They stood a few minutes and listened as one and another spoke of deliverance from sin and fear, and of having heart peace. Was this what she needed? If she joined some church or other, Tenrikyo or some other sect, would she escape the sense of guilt and of condemnation that so often gripped her soul when she was alone? So Sumi thought both then and later on as they hurried back to the dormitory.

Her time, however, in Kobe was coming to an end. As the summer came on she contracted pleurisy and beriberi, possibly owing to the poor living conditions and plain food in the dormitory. Her condition was bad enough for her to go to hospital, and there she stayed for three months. The letters from home betrayed their anxiety for her, but money was too scarce for her parents to make the journey to visit her. She also learned that Kazuo had been called to the colours and had joined the army in Hiroshima. War was in the air and Japan was sending troops to China. She dreaded the thought that Kazuo might eventually land there, but she could do nothing but hope for the best. Even if she went home he would not be there now. The village would be duller without him.

At length her health began to return, but the mill doctor would not pass her for further work in her weakened condition. So she said goodbye to her workmates, and when the ripening rice was waving in the fields she stepped off the bus in her home village.

"Sumi, honourably return."

"O honourable mother, I have just come back. How are you?"

"Why, Sumi, what has happened to you? You are so thin and your face colour is so pale," and honourable mother could not restrain the tears that flowed down her cheeks.

"Mother, do not cry! The work was hard and the hours long, and I tried so hard to study at school. The food too was very poor. But now I am home, and with your cooking I shall soon be fat again."

And so it proved to be. A few weeks and Sumi's health was fully restored and her cheeks glowed with colour, even if deep down in her heart the sense of guilt remained unallayed.

.   .   .   .   .

To those in Japan who know nothing but the nebulous, traditional teaching of Buddhism, man is like a chip of wood swept along on the stream of life. Now passing through the rapids of trouble where the turbulent water dashes over the rocks, now finding temporary rest in the quiet waters of some smiling pool. Yet again hurried along willy-nilly on the flood-tide, at last to find endless peace in the great tranquil ocean of Nirvana. It is all a matter of luck, of chance, of fate, though man may by much effort do something to mitigate his circumstances, if not to change the course of his destiny.

The Christian believes in a divine plan, a God who orders all according to His perfect will, with man finding his highest bliss in conformity to that will. Sumi San little knew it at the time, but she was soon to make a decision that affected the whole trend of her life, and who shall deny that God was behind it? Because of the choice she made she was led into paths of great suffering, and because of it she found a sphere of service which under the blessing of God brought great joy to her soul and eternal fruit to her reward. But that is to anticipate the story.

During her weeks at home she had busied herself learning home weaving and dressmaking, but it was obvious that these did not bring money into the needy family. So when she learned of vacancies for students in the Hiroshima Nurses' School she made application to enter. She was not only successful but able to enter on scholarship, which considerably cut essential expenses. So once again she left Funo village and made her way into the outside world. Once again dormitory life was the order of the day, but she was a student now and thoroughly enjoyed the technical studies and the practical work in the adjoining hospital. She came face to face with death now in all its ugliness, and she had no answer in her own soul for its grim loneliness.

In her spare time there were cultural activities arranged for the girls. She enjoyed learning the art of flower arrangement and the way to perform the tea ceremony with poise and decorum. The classes were conducted in the dormitory by a Buddhist nun, and Sumi was rather attracted to her. The nun, too, saw in Sumi San a bright young woman of keen intelligence, and from time to time they chatted together about life and its problem. Flower arrangement and the tea ceremony might bring a measure of serenity to the mind, but they could not satisfy the longing in Sumi's soul.

"You have been given great gifts, Sumi San, and you must develop them yourself. None of us is without some good quality, but Hotoke San has especially favoured you. You must cultivate the Buddha within you, let the good grow and increase to the exclusion of the evil. Repudiate unworthy thoughts, put forth all your effort to achieve what is noble. Learn the Buddhist scriptures and fill your mind with them. So will you succeed in life and achieve enlightenment hereafter."

The time in the school passed quickly and Sumi San did well in her studies. She hardly expected to excel as she did, but when she finally graduated she was honours student for the whole of Hiroshima Prefecture. It was with a joyful heart that she left the school and entered the Nurses' Home connected with the hospital. Now she would be able to work and earn money and soon the debts incurred during her student years would be paid off.

She had just come off night duty one morning when one of the staff in the office came up to her.

"Are you Sumi San and is your surname Takagi?" she asked.

"Yes, that's right!"

"Then there is a wire for you," and she handed her the folded paper. What could this mean? Who could be sending her a telegram?

"Return at once. Mother dangerously ill," she read with quivering lips and failing courage.

Her course of action was clear. She must go home. So, obtaining permission from the matron, she left as soon as she could, her mind filled with misgivings. The words of the telegram seemed to be echoed by the train as it hurried along the rails—"Return at once, mother ill. Return at once, mother ill." At length, exhausted, she fell into a doze.

She awoke to find herself at her destination. Yes, there was the bus for home. On to the bus. Through the villages, along the narrow roads. Ah, here is my stop. Up the street, into the house.

"I have just returned."

"Ah, Sumi, is it you? Honourably return! You have done well to come so soon—and yet you are too late. Mother has died!"

She could not answer at once, and the tears welled up unsummoned and flowed unchecked. What cruel blow of fate was this, just when she had graduated and was getting into the work of nursing? Mother gone, and who indeed could take her place? Sumi had met death in the hospital, but there it seemed apart from her. Here it was in her very home. Was she wicked that this thing had happened to her? Could it be that her own sin had brought this tragedy upon the family?

The grief coupled with physical tiredness temporarily overwhelmed her, but in a while she recovered. There was much to do. She was mother now, the oldest in the family. On her largely rested responsibility for the care of her brothers aged seventeen, twelve and eight years. So throughout the funeral preparations and the final rites Sumi was composed and strong.

When the funeral was over a gathering of the relatives was held to discuss the future of Takagi San and his family. There were still debts to be paid, and added to these was the fresh debt incurred by Sumi San's training as a nurse. At the time of her graduation everything seemed so rosy. She would soon earn the needed money at her nursing to pay her training expenses, and then from her steady income be able to help pay off the family debts. Now once more it seemed as though Takagi and his children were back where they had started.

The discussion went back and forth among the relatives without much progress being made until at length an uncle made a suggestion. He came from a place just over the border in Shimane Prefecture and had quite a large lumber business. They all knew he had money and if for no other reason his advice carried weight. He cleared his throat and said:

"I think we should do what we can to encourage Sumi in her nursing. She has studied hard and graduated first in the whole of Hiroshima Prefecture. If she stays here now how is she going to use her nursing—I suppose there is already a nurse in the village—and how is she going to help out with the family debt? So I'm going to make an offer. If you, Takagi, will let her carry on her nursing in Hiroshima, or Kobe, if you like, I'll pay all the expenses she incurred while in training."

A murmur of voices rose from the gathered relatives, with Takagi and Sumi San bowing low and saying, "No, no, on no account. We will never hear of it. We'll manage through somehow."

However, it was obvious that they were both grateful and delighted. So it was decided that Sumi San should stay at home for a year until the first anniversary of her mother's death should be commemorated. Then she was to take up nursing again. By that time also arrangements could be made for the care of the family in her absence. Sumi San was overjoyed as she went to sleep that night, though her joy was tinged with the pain of her mother's death. Hotoke San was caring for her. He would see her through.

The time went by quickly. Soon arrangements were being made for the memorial of her mother's death held on the forty-ninth day. The uncle who had paid her expenses came over and relatives and neighbours came in. The little casket containing her mother's remains was brought out and suitably placed among the borrowed Buddhist ornaments. On the top a photograph of her mother was placed, illuminated by lighted candles, and across it drifted from time to time the smoke from the sweet-smelling incense. The friends gathered in a circle round the shrine and with clanging sistra moaned through the Buddhist scriptures suitable for the occasion. Sumi San, sitting in a corner, felt the wound in her heart opening again and furtively wiped the falling tear with the corner of her kimono sleeve. Within the hour the ceremony was over and food was brought out. Then everybody engaged in almost unseemly good-neighbourly mirth and conversation, before bowing politely and going out into the night.

Chapter 3

GOLD GLEAMS IN THE ORE

THE year at home was nearing its end when Sumi began to make arrangements for continuing her nursing career. She had kept up her studies and now felt she could earn better money and have greater freedom if she joined a district nursing association. Hiroshima, while a provincial town, did not offer much scope in this line, so Sumi naturally thought again of Kobe, which she already knew in some measure. Eventually, after some correspondence, she joined a District Nurses' Association in the eastern part of Kobe and eagerly anticipated starting work there.

Kobe at that time was a port city of nearly one million people, lying between the mountains and the sea in a coastal plain up to three miles wide at its widest part. Stretching from the port centre east and west were dwelling houses and shops, with many small factories engaged in making, among other things, rubber and celluloid goods, machinery parts, and later, when war in China started, shell-cases, small arms and the like. In the west the city terminated in Suma Park and the historically famous Ichinotani. In the east the city thinned out into the plain stretching to the city of Osaka. Sumiyoshi, where Sumi San found her nursing headquarters, was a good spot to live in as the meaning of its Japanese name implied. Behind was Mount Rokko with its twin cable-car routes, its hanging rope-way, and wide curving motor-road reaching to the summit. Before were the blue waters of Osaka Bay, with the breakwaters of Kobe Harbour reaching out to embrace part of the sea for the port's own use. A trip to the summit of Rokko provided the climber with a splendid view and, in summertime, with some respite from the steaming heat and stuffy smell of the teeming city.

When Sumi San reached Kobe, however, the worst of the heat was over, though September brought the threat of typhoons. She soon settled down to work, busying herself daily with the dressing of wounds and the care of the sick. Bad ears, bad eyes, sore arms, sore legs; pains in the stomach, pains in the head. There seemed no end to it. What would it be like in the winter? Sumi San worked faithfully and happily, and her kind words of encouragement helped more than one of her patients. She was doing well financially too, and month by month was able to send money home. Thrift was a strong point with Sumi San, and she kept regular account of her income and expenditure. Everything she could spare found its way to Funo village.

In this way several happy years passed. Sumi was happy in her work and feeling that she was fulfilling her vocation in life. Then one day she was called to a rather better-class house in Mikage, a residential area of East Kobe. A little boy was ill with an ulcerated leg, and Sumi San was called to give him attention. The wound proved a very stubborn one, and it was soon evident to the nurse that the bone itself was diseased. So her visits to the Komatsu home became almost a regular part of her daily life. The boy was a bright young chap in spite of his sore leg and enforced inactivity.

"Hallo, Machan, how are you today? Still nursing your leg?"

"Yes, nurse, still here. See what I've got—an aeroplane. I'm going to get honourable father to hang it from the ceiling just above my head. Then I can push it round and round. It's a fighter plane like our airmen use."

"My, isn't it splendid! Now let's look at that leg, and you be just as brave as our soldiers while I change the dressing."

"Okay, nurse, go ahead, I'll be brave."

Sometimes nurse took the little fellow something herself. A little Santa Claus as Christmas and its commercialised festivity approached. A box of candies at the New Year, for it was Machan's leg, not his appetite, that was impaired. As spring came round one day Sumi San took him a lovely branch of cherry blossom just about in full bloom.

"Morning, Machan! 'Spring has come, Where do you think that spring has come?' " said Sumi San, as she sung the lines of a well-known children's song.

The little fellow caught on at once and sang in reply:

" 'On the mountains, in the valleys, spring has come at last!' Oh, thank you, nurse, how lovely! I'll get mother to put it in a vase, and then I'll be able to go flower-viewing right here in my quilts."

"Hallo, what's going on here?" The voice was that of a man.

"Honourably return, daddy. Look what nurse has brought. Isn't it beautiful!"

"It certainly is lovely. Thank you, nurse, very much. I don't know how we can thank you enough for all you've done for our boy here. You've not only faithfully dressed his wounds but you've cheered up his spirits time and again. Your daily visits have been quite an institution and you yourself seem one of the family. Could you stay with us for lunch today?"

Komatsu San was a typical middle-class Japanese man. He was of medium height, with fairly full face, and he had reached that age where his form was spreading comfortably into the hitherto unexplored areas of his tweed suit. His job at the shipbuilding yards was at any rate secure, for Japan's trade was booming and her ships were carrying goods throughout the world. He enjoyed his home and his only child. Here again was security—a wife to cook and handle domestic affairs, to lay out his clothes when business called him to journey, to greet him with almost docile faithfulness on his return. That did not mean he could not have his fling, as he did once in a while. The men from the company would make up a party and spend a couple of days at Shirahama hot-spring. The women there catered only too well for the city men. The *sake* flowed freely then and at other times—to drink and to smoke, were these not commonplace among men all over Japan! It could hardly be said that Tokieda's face showed evidences of debauchery. Shall we say that it showed a predilection for the so-called good life. Probably it was his boy more than anything else that gave him real love, so it was all the more a blow to him when what had seemed to be an ordinary sore had developed into tuberculosis of the leg bone. But this little nurse had done a good job, a very good job, and the boy was at last on the upgrade.

"Could you stay and have lunch with us today?" He repeated his invitation. "I happen to have the afternoon off from the company, and I know Machan would like to keep you here a little longer."

"Thank you very much, but I still have a few calls to make this morning and more this afternoon. It is very kind of you."

"That's too bad. Some other time, eh?"

"It is very kind of you. Now I must go, if you will excuse me. Goodbye, Machan!"

It was Komatsu San himself who followed her to the porch and saw her off. He returned saying to himself, "A good nurse, a very fine nurse indeed!"

It was the insistence of Machan as much as anything else that prompted Sumi San to accept a later invitation to a meal at Komatsu's house. From the point of view of her nursing service it was better not to become too friendly with her clients. But this was different, a little boy and an only, lonely son, and she could not but comply with the repeated requests. Sumi went once, twice, several times, and was glad of the friendliness of the home. It made a change from the Nurses' Home.

At length the boy was better and no longer needed the attention of the nurse. It had been a long time, ten successive months of illness, but at last the wound was closed and Machan was on his feet again, taller, but thinner than when he had fallen sick. Sumi San was in the home for the last visit, and Machan had surprised her with a beautifully wrapped package.

"Nurse, this is just a very little, useless thing, but I'd like you to have it. You've been so good to me."

"No, Machan, no thank you! I've only been doing my job like any other nurse, and it has been good to meet a brave little fellow like you. I couldn't accept a thing!"

"Oh, please do. It's not very much, and it will remind you of Komatsu Masashige when you go to other places. Do accept it, please."

"Yes, nurse, Machan wants you to have it: please accept it." It was the father who spoke. Sumi knew he was at home on two or three days' holiday, but she had imagined he was out somewhere.

"Very well then, but really I only did my job. Thank you, Machan, very much. Now be a good boy and take care not to get any kicks on that leg at school. Goodbye."

"Okay, nurse, goodbye, and take care of yourself."

Komatsu San accompanied her to the door.

"Nurse, I don't know how we can thank you for all you've done for Machan. We feared he might not recover at first, but you have pulled him through to health and strength. All we have to do now is to feed him up a bit. We are most grateful."

"Not at all. I have only done my job and have enjoyed meeting Machan. Thank you for having me round so many times."

"Oh, that's nothing. Nurse, I have one request to make before you go."

"What is it?"

"Will you meet me tomorrow evening at Sannomiya Station? I want to have a private talk with you."

Sumi San was taken aback by this request. It was unusual, to say the least of it. What did Komatsu San want to see her about? Was it something to do with her nursing or with the future health of the boy? But then he need not be secretive about that. A private talk was hardly called for. If she refused to go perhaps it would show ingratitude. The family had been kind to her, and even now she was carrying away a present from them. She was virtually under an obligation to go. In any case Sannomiya Station was a bright public place and no harm could come if she did meet him. So she found herself consenting.

"I'm very busy, but I think I could make time if it is very important. What time?"

"About seven o'clock all right for you, nurse? I wouldn't trouble you, but it is rather important."

"All right then, seven o'clock. Good morning."

Chapter 4

A DARK VEIN IS INTRODUCED

SANNOMIYA Station is a busy place, not unknown to the many foreign tourists who visit the city of Kobe. The broad, straight road that leads up from the docks runs under the elevated government railway line at the station. In the adjacent departmental store a private electric line has its terminus, and there the express trains come to rest after hurtling along from Osaka in twenty-five minutes. Normally, the buildings near Sannomiya are bright with garish neon signs, but an abnormally dry period had led to restrictions in the use of electricity, and the area was dimmer than usual. There was, however, no restricting the gay life in the narrow streets that wound in and out of the area.

Sumi San was on time at the appointed rendezvous, and after a few minutes Komatsu San appeared.

"Ah, good evening, nurse. Hope I haven't kept you waiting."

"No, I came just a few minutes ago."

"Good. Now look, we can't talk privately here, so let us go and have a drink of something cool and talk there."

So saying, Komatsu San walked off, with the nurse following a couple of steps behind. In and out the narrow streets, by places where tinny gramophones did little to commend the invention of Thomas Edison, and where voices were upraised in ribald singing. At length they stopped before a large Japanese-style building and went in. A chorus of voices intoned "Welcome!", and one waitress separated herself from the group to lead Komatsu into the building. It was evident that he was known to the proprietors. He chose a little cubicle detached from the main part of the restaurant.

"Here, this will do. We can talk quietly here. What will you drink? No beer, I guess. Lemonade? All right." And the drinks were ordered.

But Sumi San was ill at ease. She knew enough from the

type of waitress that welcomed them and the splendid appointments of the building to realise this was a *ryōriya*. To give it the direct English translation of "restaurant" or "eating-house" sounds innocuous enough. But many a Japanese would raise his eyebrows at the word, and what respectable man would wish his daughters to serve in such a place? Sumi San's fears were not without foundation.

"You'll be wondering why I have brought you here, nurse. As a matter of fact I want to say once again how grateful I am for all you have done for Machan these past months. When I first heard that his leg bone was diseased I felt all was hopeless. If he did not die, at least he would be a helpless cripple for the rest of his life, and, as you know, he is my heir and indeed my only child. You have done more than nurse him back to health and strength, you have brought new confidence to me too. The boy is well, and I am restored from the sense of depression and frustration that had settled upon me. We looked forward to your visits and your cheery smile. While you sought to cheer up Machan you cheered me up and encouraged me too. So I want to say a grateful thank-you to you. And would you please accept this as a token of my appreciation."

Komatsu slipped a thin, white paper packet across the table to where Sumi San sat with downcast eyes. It was ceremoniously tied with red and white cord and written upon with suitable characters. Sumi San knew it was a gift of money.

"It is very kind of you, but I cannot accept your gift. The Nursing Association pays me for my services, and I have done nothing more than my job. Please don't think about a gift for me. It will only make me embarrassed. It is very rude of me, but . . ."

And Sumi San pushed the packet back.

Komatsu was determined, however, and at length the packet was in Sumi's possession, though she was ill at ease about the whole matter.

"There's one more thing. Sumi San"—he used her own name now—"I want to see you sometimes. You have been such a help to me in giving me a lift on the way, that I'd like to have a chat with you when I'm down. We'd like to have you over for an evening at the house now and again too."

"I am a debtor to your kindness, Mr. Komatsu, but I cannot fall in with your suggestion. In any case a poor nurse like I am can do nothing to help you. I shall be too busy to meet you again."

Sumi San put on a bold front though her heart was thumping with fear and apprehension.

"Aw, don't turn me down like that. I'm not asking much. Just to have a chat once in a while and get a little lift along the way. Surely you can do that for me?"

We need not follow the conversation to the end. It would be easy to say that the nurse was weak-willed, but she was already under an obligation to the man, on more than one count. Her Japanese background taught her that indebtedness must be paid off in no lesser degree than the debt incurred. Komatsu San had played his game well; first the gifts and then the request. It was a mild form of blackmail. Before they left the building Sumi San had agreed in a half-hearted way to "have a chat once in a while". She was determined that it should be nothing more than that. What she could not know was the measure in which Komatsu would exploit the situation.

Back in her room at the Nurses' Home Sumi San opened the packet. One hundred yen! More than she could earn in two months as a nurse! This was big money, and how great was her indebtedness—how indeed could she discharge the obligation she had incurred in receiving it? What should she do? In a moment of panic she thought she would run to the police-box at the corner and hand it in. But then what could she say, how could she explain the matter? No, that would not do! Her heart sank as she realised how strong was the bond that held her. Take it back, send it back! But Komatsu would not receive it, and anyway how could she be so rude and ungrateful? There was nothing for it but to keep it, and perhaps later send it home. They could use it there.

Her sleep that night was restless. It seemed as if the spectre of the moral failure in Yamaguchi had taken on a new form and threatened her again. Why should it pursue her here, and just when she was so happy in her work? She was doing what she could to use her talents, to help others, to spread good-will as the Buddhist nun had taught her. Why then this intrusion of her old failure? Could she never get away from it, or was her whole life to be blighted by this thing?

She was awake early, and as she saw things in a clearer light she felt sure she should leave Kobe as soon as possible. But where should she go? Somewhere where she could continue nursing and where she could be far away from Komatsu and his advances. Her mind was made up; she would, she must go.

It took a few weeks to find other work, but at length arrangements were completed for Sumi to go to Tokyo. She was to enter a District Nurses' Home there and continue with much the same work as she had been doing in Kobe. Komatsu had seen her several times during those few weeks, much to Sumi San's discomfiture. However, it would soon be over, and in the great metropolis she would be lost and able to continue her work in peace. She had to tell him she was going, and with that disclosure the break was made.

.   .   .   .   .

The "Swallow" express, in those days, steamed out of Kobe station every morning sharp at 9 a.m., making the journey to Tokyo in eight and a half hours. It was a lovely morning as Sumi San stood on the platform awaiting the arrival of the train. There was an off-shore wind and the mountains behind the city were clear against the blue sky. She breathed in the fresh air. Soon—ah, so soon now—she would be clear of the muddling mists that had confused her during her last weeks in Kobe. Like the mountains, she too, cleansed and freed, would reach up to higher heights of usefulness.

"Good morning, Sumi San. An early start, eh?"

Sumi San turned round to face Komatsu, whose smile showed the least suspicion of a sneering curl at the corners of his mouth.

"What are you doing here? Are you going too? You have a ticket, I see." Sumi was filled with amazement and trepidation.

"Yes, I'm coming too—as far as Kyoto! You don't think I could let a kind friend go away without any send-off, do you? You have done so much for me and the family. Machan sends his greetings and would have been here but for school. You would sooner I hadn't come?"

Evidently Sumi's thoughts were reflected in her face—not that Komatsu could or would be so easily repelled.

"Why, er . . . I did not expect to see you. You surprised me. Greet Machan for me and tell him to keep hard at his studies. Here is the train. Goodbye, I must go!"

"Sumi San, just this once. Let me see you off as far as Kyoto."

She gave no answer, and none was expected. Komatsu was on the train too and the departure bell was already ringing.

Sumi San was silent in her fear and concern during the early part of the journey, but there was one ray of hope. She was going away from it all, and if she could put up with Komatsu until they reached Kyoto she would be rid of him for ever. After all, he was a married man with a family and had no business approaching her the way he did.

"So you're not going to talk? Here have I come all the way to see you off and you are as silent as the grave. Can't you be friendly for the last hour?"

"Komatsu San, I will speak frankly. I appreciate all your kindness and am greatly indebted to you. But you are a married man, and you must be true to your wife and to Machan. So please do not trouble me any more. In any case I hope to marry Kazuo San back home—when he is released from the army."

"Oh, that's it, is it? A boy-friend back home. Listen, Kazuo can't do for you half as much as I can. . . ."

"Komatsu San," she interrupted, "please say no more. I am going to Tokyo and I want to . . . I want to forget all about you."

The man was rebuffed, and the farewell at Kyoto was cold, though of necessity outwardly polite. Sumi San settled back in the seat as the train started off again, pulling heavily up through the twin tunnels that lie east of Kyoto. Soon they were skirting the shores of Lake Biwa, the largest lake in Japan, and passing under the shadow of Mount Ibuki. A brief stop was made at the great city of Nagoya with its famous castle adorned with golden dolphins, and in the afternoon Mount Fuji could be seen towering into the clear sky. On the train sped, and as the sun sank in the west Sumi San set her eyes for the first time on Japan's huge metropolis of Tokyo.

.   .   .   .   .

We may pass quickly over the early days in Tokyo. The Nurses' Home was in the suburb of Shiba, not very far from Shina Park with its great temple Zojoji. Her work often took her through the park, and she would then stop to mutter a prayer before the Buddha housed beneath the temple's expansive roof. She was happily busy and gradually the horrible fears of the Kobe days passed away.

Sumi San was one to make progress. She was always keen to better herself. So it came about at length that she left the Nursing Association and took up work at a private hospital. As a District Nurse she had been on call even at night and had little time for study, and she was anxious to complete the High School course she had started while at the Kobe factory. The hospital work gave her more regular hours, and she was able to go to school again. She soon found, however, that the studies were more difficult than she had anticipated; she had forgotten she was now a few years older. So, at length abandoning her night-school studies, she started lessons instead at a midwifery school. This was definitely more to her liking and in line with her daily work. She did well at her studies and in due course graduated and received her diploma. Now she was qualified both for general nursing and midwifery. She wrote to Kazuo San in China to tell him of her new success, but no reply came. Was he safe? Would he be in the danger zone where fierce fighting was going on? There was nothing and no one to re-assure her.

It must have been some months, if not a year or more after she had arrived in Tokyo that Sumi San's steady progress was arrested and she was again cast back into the midst of the gripping fears from which she had sought to escape. She was living in her own room a short distance from the hospital where she was employed, and walked over each morning to work. This particular morning as she entered the hospital the girl in the office said:

"Good morning, Sumi San. Did you see your friend?"

"Friend? No! Did someone come for me?"

"Yes, about half an hour ago a gentleman called here to see you. Said he knew you well, so I sent him over to your rooms."

"Is that so? I guess he must have gone a different way and so we did not meet. I'll just see the doctor and ask if I can get off for an hour or so."

The hospital was not very busy, and Sumi had the time granted to her. So she made her way back to her room. Who could it be wanting to see her here in Tokyo? "Couldn't be

Kazuo San, I suppose? But then he would be in uniform, unless he had been discharged," she reasoned in her heart.

She opened the door into the porch, and at once the woman of the house came out.

"Honourably return, Takagi San. One of your relatives has come to see you from your native place. He said he had called at the hospital and they sent him on here. As I knew you would be back as soon as you heard that he had come, I showed him up to your room."

"Thank you. That was very kind of you."

Sumi San made her way upstairs, opened the sliding paper doors into her room, and looked into the face of Komatsu San.

"Good morning, Sumi San. It is quite a while since I saw you."

"Komatsu San, what are you doing here?" gasped Sumi San. She felt weak and sank to her knees on the soft straw-matted floor.

Komatsu laughed. "Ha, you are surprised; you didn't expect to see me. Did you think I had forgotten you?"

"But how did you find me? How did you get my address?" countered Sumi San.

"That was easy. They knew your address at the Kobe Nurses' Home and gladly gave it to me. When I arrived in Tokyo I found you had left the District Nurses' Association, but they kindly"—he almost sneered—"directed me to the hospital, and here I am."

"But what do you want with me, Komatsu San? Why did you come to Tokyo?" continued Sumi San.

"I came on business—business with you."

"You have nothing to do with me, Komatsu San, and I would far sooner you had not come." It was fear of this determined man that made Sumi bold, but his reasonableness disarmed her.

"Sumi San, please listen. I have journeyed a long way to have a friendly sensible talk with you, and I want you to listen. Be good enough to hear what I have to say and then you can make your own decisions. I know you have your work to attend to this morning, and I actually have a few calls I want to make. Let me come this evening and chat with you. Machan is fine and well and wanted to send his greetings to you. He'll soon be going into Middle School. How well you served us when he was ill. You were indeed a friend to our family, and my suggestion is an endeavour to repay your kindness to us. Will you listen to me this evening?"

His speech was suave and almost reassuring. Perhaps the man had changed and repented of his temporary infatuation. She could but listen to him. So Sumi San agreed to meet him again in her room that evening when her day's work was done.

The meeting with Komatsu San that evening recalled in some measure the time they met in the eating-house near Sannomiya. Sumi San found herself fervently hoping that the outcome of the present interview would not disturb her peace of mind as the previous one had done.

"Sumi San, I come this evening to speak to you as a friend. You will be surprised to know that I have been to your home in Funo village and met your father and relatives there."

He paused for the statement to sink in and take due effect. Sumi San was obviously surprised, and even more puzzled as to why he should have visited her native place.

"You are no doubt wondering why I went. Well, as I said, we sort of look upon you as a friend of the family, and I felt I could arrange a good and suitable marriage for you. No, don't interrupt me; please listen. You are now twenty-seven—or eight, is it?—and at that age it will become increasingly difficult for you to get married. So I took it upon myself to make a suggestion to your father, although I realise it was very rude of me. The person in question is my younger brother Jiro, and both your relatives and I feel it would be a good match. They were very pleased to think that you could be married to the brother of, shall I say, a prosperous Kobe business man. Excuse me talking of myself in this way. So with their agreement obtained all we need now is your own personal consent."

Marriages are arranged by intermediaries in Japan and Sumi was quite well acquainted with the system. She was dumbfounded, however, to think that Komatsu San had used his comparatively slight acquaintance with her to propose a marriage with his younger brother. Still more to hear that he had actually obtained the consent of her relatives back home and arrived in Tokyo to present her with a *fait accompli*. She knew that Jiro lived with the Komatsus in Kobe, but he always seemed to be out of the house and she had actually never met him face to face.

"All we need now is your personal consent." Like every other Japanese girl, Sumi looked forward to marriage—sometime. Just now in a very real way she was married to her work and happy in it. The money she earned as she worked was helping the family back home. That would cease if she married now. Marriage was right and proper in its place, in its time—but not yet.

"All we need now is your personal consent." The words echoed in her mind and gripped her heart. Wait a moment! What about Kazuo San? There had been no understanding of marriage, no engagement or promises made, but they were both waiting, keeping clear of other entanglements, so that they might be married properly and discreetly in due course. Kazuo San was in China, but he would surely return. Her first loyalty was to him.

"You have travelled far and been most diligent. I appreciate all you have done for one so worthless as I am. I am sorry, however, I cannot give my consent," replied Sumi San.

"Not quite so fast, Sumi San. You must think over the matter a little more carefully. You must weigh the advantages of the marriage into a prosperous city family of you, a country girl. Such an opportunity will hardly come your way again. Think again a little more slowly."

"Komatsu San, were I to think long and carefully my reply would still be the same. I told you once before about Kazuo, and I remain loyal and true to him."

This uncompromising and firm attitude of the nurse was more than Komatsu had expected. His offer was reasonable and attractive, he thought; and having acquired the goodwill of her relatives, he had not foreseen that Sumi San would repudiate his suggestion. His smooth manner hardened, he was somewhat angry.

"Sumi San, you're unreasonable. Do you mean to say you will defy the wishes of your relatives and turn down this valuable marriage offer? I've already told them that we can put up the money to pay your family debts in one payment. Think again!"

"I'm sorry. I may appear stubborn, but I am pledged to Kazuo and I cannot accept your offer. We will work together when we are married and rid our family of debt. I don't think I want to live in a city house: I love my native hills and valleys."

Still stubborn. Still refusing. Komatsu determined to turn the screw one more turn. This would make her respond. His attitude was leering, cynical as he said:

"So you will work and pay off the debt, will you? There's another debt you must pay now. Do you think I can run up and down to Hiroshima and come up here to Tokyo at my own expense? I have only done this for your good, as a family friend, and you coolly refuse the offer of my good offices and cling to your farmer's boy. Sumi San, if you refuse to give your consent I shall take you to court until every penny of my expenses is paid. What is more, I stay in this room until you consent. It is nine o'clock now. What would your reputation as a nurse be worth if it became known that you entertained a man in your room this night? I am staying here until you say 'Yes', and you cannot escape me."

He moved over to the sliding doors as if to prevent her escape. But Sumi San was like a caged bird, weakened, beaten, with no will or power to fly. Once again her sin had caught up with her. It had hunted her from Yamaguchi to Hiroshima, from Kobe to Tokyo. She was trapped. Yet perhaps the marriage would work out all right. Would Kazuo San understand if she explained to him? After all, it was yet to be proved that a match between Kazuo and her would win the approval of the family. She had not wanted to marry yet, she had not wanted marriage forced upon her, nor had she wanted it in this way. The will of the family was important and sometimes all-powerful. It might be better to yield: indeed could she do anything else?

"I consent." Sumi San spoke with a low, trembling voice, her eyes cast down, twisting and re-twisting the wretched handkerchief she held in her hand.

"I'm glad you have become reasonable. I did not want to be hard, but, you know, you've got a stubborn streak in you." Komatsu laughed a hollow laugh. "Come, let us part good friends, for I must go. Can I tell your father you consent, and can we go ahead with the marriage plans?"

"Yes." The reply, for all it committed Sumi San for life, was non-committal in its tone.

Shortly afterwards Komatsu San left.

Chapter 5

THE BOTTOM OF THE PIT

IT soon became evident that plans for the wedding were going forward according to the normal Japanese custom. Once the bride-to-be has given her consent, arrangements are largely in the hands of the intermediaries. Soon a letter came from her home asking Sumi to return. On the way she was to meet her father in Kobe and together they would visit Komatsu's house. There for the first time she would meet her future husband and final arrangements for the wedding would be made.

Sumi was reluctant enough to leave her nursing, but there was the prospect of being able to resume it after her marriage. She was now facing the latter with more or less of joy. Marriage is anticipated by every normal Japanese girl, and her father and relatives had approved the present match. She wished it might have been marriage to Kazuo San, but then the family had agreed to the present arrangement and it would have been unfilial to disapprove. So she left the hospital and after the usual farewells made her way to Kobe, and, with her father, once again to the Komatsu home.

The interview with Jiro Komatsu was a formal affair. Both Komatsu San and his wife were there as the go-betweens, and Sumi's father and aunt represented her side of the family. Greetings were exchanged, and, as was fit and proper, Sumi San sat with downcast eyes, her hands folded on her lap. Jiro said little and seemed almost sullen, but as no objection was raised by either side the final agreements were concluded. The wedding would be held in Kobe at the Komatsu house, and married life for Sumi San would begin in the same home, to which she would go as a bride.

The ceremony itself took place a few weeks later. Until then Sumi San was happily busy at home. There were many things to get ready—quilts for use in her new home, her own kimono, and so on. Several of the neighbours called in from time to time to congratulate her on her good fortune in marrying into a prosperous city family. But then she was a nurse, they said, and was able to get about more than ordinary folk. There was one unhappiness. She learned that Kazuo San had been discharged from the army and was home again. Marriage to him was now out of the question, but she wanted to see him again for old time's sake, and to explain that the matter had been quite taken out of her hands. But news of what was pending had reached Kazuo's ears too and he refused to meet her. The pain was real if temporary, but soon the pressure of other events had moved her on and away for ever from her friend of school-days.

The wedding was in traditional Japanese style, the necessary ceremonial clothing having been borrowed for the occasion. The bride was dressed in a black silk kimono with exquisite embroidery in the front from the waist to the hem. The sash which encircled her kimono was richly embroidered in gold and silver thread. On her head Sumi San wore the customary stiff white kerchief or *tsuno kakushi* (horn covering) and her face was powdered until it was almost impossible to recognise her. The bridegroom was in morning dress, and the go-betweens were suitably dressed for the occasion. The actual ceremony was neither religious nor civil and centred around the taking of a pledge by the contracting parties. Bride and groom sat side by side before the sacred alcove, which was decorated with pine, plum and bamboo branches to signify longevity and success. Then each drank three times out of each of three wine-cups of different size, sipping the *sake* (rice-wine) nine times in all. Thus the marriage contract was sealed.

The ceremony over, congratulations were in order, and after that a wonderful feast of good things. Komatsu San was at his best, quick of wit and the soul of the party. The bridegroom of necessity was reserved until the continual round of the *sake* cup enlivened him. Then his almost wild laugh might have given one reason to question his sanity. But then he was in his cups, and it seems that almost anything can be forgiven a man when drink is his master.

The bride was, as should be, demure and silent, but glanced at him occasionally from beneath her eyelashes. What kind of a man was this to whom she was now legally bound? Jiro 'under the influence' looked almost wild, but she hastily crushed down the feeling of revulsion which rose in her heart. This was an exceptional time of course, he surely would not always be like this. Yet time and again, until the party ended and the guests departed, that half-wild laugh echoed through the room.

And now Sumi San was alone in the Komatsu house, committed to it for life, and the day which should have brought her abounding joy found her with her heart once more filled with apprehension. She struggled against the sense of misgiving. This, she told herself, was the natural result of leaving her home and loved ones to marry a man she scarcely knew: she would soon get used to her new surroundings. This was a perfectly natural reaction after the weeks of preparation and of being keyed up for the great occasion: she would feel better when she was more rested. But Sumi's fears were not unfounded, and she found, to her dismay and horror, that Jiro Komatsu, the man she had taken as her husband, was an idiot! He had his periods of sanity, but at other times was completely lunatic!

This, then, was the prosperous business man to marry whom was such a stroke of luck! She had given up her nursing to marry a half-wit! Sumi San's heart sank within her. Where was there release from this bondage? A Japanese woman in those days had no recourse to divorce. Sumi San condemned to be the plaything of a lunatic. Once again fate had caught up with her. Dogged by the sin of her youth, hounded by her fate, could she never be forgiven in this world or the next? This was the end, this was the lowest abyss; from here there was no redemption.

But why had Ichiro Komatsu arranged this marriage for her? Purely to get his idiot brother married off his hands by some means or other? At first it seemed so, but soon his real motives became evident.

The idiot Jiro was seldom in the house, and Sumi San at length found out where he spent his time. Kobe, like other large cities, has its red-light district, and it was in Fukuhara that he found his friends and associates. The Prodigal Son in his worst stage of profligacy could not have been more reprobate than Jiro. Wine, women and song were the order of the day. Sometimes, when rolling round the district half-drunk, he would join the crowd listening to a Christian preacher outside the Mission Hall on Shinkaichi. Dwarfed by the huge theatre standing next to it, the Mission Hall was none the less a light for God in that dark and sordid neighbourhood. On one such occasion it was a short, stocky student from Tokyo named Honda who was telling of new life in Christ; of the power to conquer sin and temptation, and to live holily in the midst of a sinful world. But Jiro was not ready to heed and believe. He had not yet "spent all", so he turned away and went to the gay quarters behind the Mission Hall, and continued to seek to satisfy his soul with the empty husks offered there.

Meanwhile, at home Sumi San spent her days in utter misery. This was like a living death, with neither relief in the present nor hope for the future. Bound to a hopeless profligate, not to mention a lunatic, with no hope of divorce or release of any kind. But wait, there is a way of release—at least so thought Sumi San in her unenlightened heathen mind. Death would bring deliverance from her immediate circumstances, and fate might be kinder to her in another life. She had been the victim of sin rather than its perpetrator. Conveniently enough, the railway line ran not far from the Komatsu house. Just the courage to take the step and all would be oblivion. Pain would be momentary.

But Sumi San thought again. She would be the only one to benefit by suicide. What about the family back home? The money promised and paid in part by the Komatsu family would stop if she ended her life. What a scandal too for it to be known that she had dishonoured her family by suicide. If her going would relieve others of embarrassment, or make their burden light, it would be right and honourable to take her life. But her motive, she reasoned, was purely selfish. She therefore abandoned the idea.

About this time Ichiro, the older Komatsu, began to visit Sumi San in the annexe where she lived. The continual absence of his brother and the fact that Sumi was alone made this only too easy. His true colours were now revealed. It became evident that his main purpose in arranging the marriage between Sumi and his brother was that he might have the nurse near him—for his own satisfaction! How she hated his sly under-handedness, his pursuit of her through the years, and from place to place! How she loathed his advances, and how helpless she was to resist!

Things reached a climax one night when Ichiro San forcibly molested her. Sumi San shrieked with all her might as she fought off the vicious attack. Her crying had the desired effect for from the neighbouring house an older brother of Komatsu came running in.

"What's going on here! Ichiro, what are you doing in this room?" he cried out, and it was all too evident what evil was going on. "Get out of here at once! What's all this about, Sumi San?"

As the wretched Ichiro left the room like a cur with its tail between its legs Sumi San told her story to the elder brother. The tears streamed down her face, and between her sobs she told of her wretched, sordid existence. Here at last was someone who would listen and in whom she could confide. He listened patiently and then said:

"Sumi San, I've had my suspicions of this for some time, but of course this is not my house and I have no say in the running of it. I only came in this evening because I heard you scream and thought you were in danger. I feel deeply ashamed that this should have happened to you in the home of my own younger brother, and I accept personally the responsibility for his wickedness. Now let me do what I can to make amends. The best thing you can do is to get right away from here and hide for a while; then perhaps things will better themselves. I know where you can get a room down by the shore. You will be safe there, and none but I shall know of your hiding-place."

"Elder brother, you are very kind. I owe my life to you. I cannot, I simply cannot stay here any longer, and I dare not go home. So I will accept your offer and go away. But what shall I do now? I dare not remain here another night."

"I've thought of that. You shall stay in my house this evening, and tomorrow, before anyone is about, you will be gone!"

There was a strange sense of security in Sumi San's heart that night as she rested in the elder brother's house. He was of a different type from his younger brothers and with him Sumi felt herself in safeguard. Before dawn she was up and, following the elder brother, made her way through the silent streets down towards the shores of Osaka Bay. There the houses were built close together and the streets narrower than uptown. The elder brother stopped before a single-storied building separated from the sea by a group of gnarled and twisted pine trees.

"This is the place. You will be safe here," he said as he pushed open the door. As he called out "Good morning" a kindly-faced woman of middle years came to the door and a conversation followed for some minutes. It was carried on in subdued tones and Sumi San could catch no more than a word or two.

"Come in, Sumi San. Meet Yamada San, who will be your landlady here. She is alone, for her husband died a few years ago. You are to have a six-mat room here, and I know you will find it a good home."

Greetings were exchanged, the elder brother left, and Sumi San took up residence with widow Yamada. For the most part her situation was pleasant enough, but do what she would she could not expel from her mind the hatred she felt for Ichiro San. Her own husband Jiro was a ne'er-do-well wretch, bound in vice and profligacy. He probably could not help himself. But this Ichiro with his calculated planning and evil intention—oh how she hated him. Her whole being shuddered at the thought of him. Life might be easier, it might even right itself if he were out of the way. As long as he were alive she could never return to her own home; indeed there was always the lurking fear he might even find out her hiding-place.

Yamada San was very kind, not the least in that she asked no questions. This emboldened Sumi San to tell her a little of her own heart-ache and suffering.

"I know someone who can help you, Sumi San. A friend of mine, Koide San, goes to a Christian church. Some people call it Yasu-kyo and laugh at it, saying it is a foreign religion. But certainly if it makes people like Koide San there must be something in it. Have a talk with her next time she comes to see me."

Sumi San could not have cared less about religion as such after all she had suffered. Fate was against her, the gods were unfair—indeed it seemed she had angered them in some way or other. Still, when Koide San visited the house a few days later Sumi San met her and they chatted together. Koide San was a married lady of middle age, quietly composed and genuinely happy.

"I understand you have experienced much trouble, Komatsu San, although you seem to be still quite young. My life too was filled with suffering until I believed on Jesus Christ. He says, 'Come unto me, all ye that labour and are heavy laden, and I will give you rest.' He certainly has done that for me and has lifted the burden of sin and suffering from my heart. I'm sure Christ could lift your heavy burdens and give you a life of joy instead of sorrow."

"Thank you, Koide San, but nothing can help me. The gods are against me, and fate is unkind. I've tried hard to live uprightly and help others, but every time I am on the verge of success, and feel I am of some use in the world, my destiny catches up with me and I am plunged again into distress. It is my fate, and I must resign myself to it. The only satisfaction I can get is by hating with all my heart those who have wronged me, and praying that the gods will bring down punishment on their heads."

"That is a terrible spirit to carry in one's heart through life. God is love, and He tells us to love our enemies. He can take that spirit of hatred out of our hearts. . . ."

"I can't believe in a God of love after all I've suffered," interrupted Sumi San. "If He loves me why have I been plunged into such awful experiences? No, you are wrong. Fate is blind and cruel, and hatred of those who have wronged me shall be my daily food and drink. With this I will satisfy my heart."

Koide San could see that further discussion was useless, but she warmed toward the crushed and dispirited young wife and carried her upon her heart in prayer before the God who is truly love.

.   .   .   .   .

The solitary soul nurses his own grievance. He spends his waking hours looking into his own heart and commiserating with his lot, and his dreams at night are filled with visions of the same. The conviction increases that he has been wronged, and that society has conspired against him, the innocent victim. Introspection breeds distortion. The smallest thing— a word remembered, an action recalled—is magnified out of all proportion, and then added to the growing pile of evidence for the victim and against his enemies. Self-pity and hate feed the image conceived in the mind till at length the soul is living in an unreal world of fantasy.

In Sumi San's case it could be justly claimed that she was indeed the victim, but the process of thought within her lonely soul followed the same pattern. "Hatred shall be my daily food and drink," she had said, and as the days went by hatred increasingly filled her heart. The gods were cruel, society was unkind and had cast her out, her husband was an imbecile load upon her back, and over the whole, reigning as some arch-fiend, was Ichiro. How she hated him and longed for his destruction! How often, in the chambers of her mind, she pictured his violent death!

One night when all was quiet she contrived to slip quietly out of the house into the wood nearby. The moon was waning and cast its fitful gleams between the gnarled pine trees, to trace dark patterns on the ground. She made sure she was not detected and passed to a remote corner where no one could see her. It was past midnight and none was likely to pass. The fishermen retired early and were off before dawn to their fishing. The sea swished softly as it lapped the beach, and in the distance the deep note of a temple bell echoed through the night. Reaching her objective, Sumi San took from the fold of her sash a white card and affixed it to one of the trees about breast-high from the ground. It was a photograph—a photograph of Komatsu Ichiro, the burden of her hate and venom. Next she drew from her long sleeves a small Japanese hand-towel and two candles. She knotted the towel round her head in such a way that she was able to fix in it the two candles, which she had previously lighted. They stood upright from her head for all the world like two fiery horns. A long sharp instrument that looked like a big nail or a small stiletto completed her preparations. There in the pine forest she stood, the flickering candles etching her distraught face in light and shade till she looked like the high-priestess of some evil cult.

And now she stood in front of the picture and folded her hands as if in prayer. Then, looking up, she began muttering and calling on all the gods she knew to send all the wrath and judgment they knew upon Komatsu Ichiro. At the same time she plunged her weapon again and again into the picture of the hated victim. She stopped; again she prayed, again she cursed, and, like one possessed, time and again attacked the picture with all her strength. Had her victim been himself before her she could hardly have given expression to her bitterness and hatred with greater vehemence. All the pent-up fury and anger of her soul poured itself out until, exhausted, she sank to the ground and, covering her face with her hands, wept and sobbed convulsively.

At length she was calm again and arose. The moon was fast setting behind the hills as she made her way back into the house. Sumi San had done what many another Japanese in similar circumstances had done. In her heathenism she had sought to invoke by magic means the wrath of the gods upon the man who had so cruelly wronged her.

Perhaps it was weeks or even months later that the news reached her and she learned that Komatsu Ichiro had become a lunatic. He was so violent in his madness that he had to be removed to an institution and there subsequently he died. Explain it as you will—magic, coincidence, a question of heredity—but do not deny that "as a man soweth so shall he also reap". "The mills of God grind slowly, but they grind exceeding small."

Chapter 6

SOLID ROCK IN SEEMING VOID

IT was some fifteen months after her marriage that Sumi San was at last able to return with safety to her own home and husband, if husband he might be called. The Manchurian Incident was assuming serious proportions and all able-bodied persons in Japan were being pressed into service. Jiro was able to do some work in his saner periods, but still continually frequented the licensed quarters, wasting his substance and strength in riotous living.

Sumi San now felt she should return to her nursing; and indeed she needed to, for with her husband's profligacy they were at all times on the verge of poverty. So she began some refresher courses of study in the spring of the year, but before she could complete them she caught pneumonia and was confined to bed for some five months. At first her condition was very serious, and in her weakened condition she felt the end was near. However, she pulled through to restored health and strength and was thereby convinced that the gods had not forsaken her.

Although she had left widow Yamada, the good woman came occasionally to see her together with Mrs. Koide, especially when they learned of her illness. The latter lost no opportunity to press upon Sumi San the claims of Christ, and often invited her to the little church in Mikage.

"Sumi San, I believe God has laid you aside just now to speak to your heart. Your circumstances have improved somewhat, and perhaps if you prosper you will cease to feel your need of Him. Some people think God is just a convenience, to give us healing of body, prosperity in business and security in our homes. But Jesus said, 'Seek ye first the kingdom of God and His righteousness and all these things will be added unto you.' The secret of true happiness in life is to put God first all the time."

49

"Do you think, then, Koide San, that your God of love is punishing me again, as if I had not suffered enough already? I think that things like illnesses and accidents just happen to us, though some people do say it is because the gods are angry."

"No, Sumi San, God is not punishing you for sin so much as chastening you to lead you to Himself. So far your heart has not responded to Him, you have been so wrapped up in your own misfortune and hurt and suffering. Now, once again He is saying, 'My daughter, give me thy heart.' You cannot find true peace without Christ living and reigning in your heart and life."

"I'm afraid I can't understand. I suppose it is because Christianity is a foreign religion."

But Koide San was always ready to pray with the sick and frustrated woman, and who shall doubt that God heard and answered.

Now better in health, Sumi returned to her beloved nursing, working as a midwife in the area where her home was situated. Joy gradually came back to her heart. She found it in forgetting herself and her own troubles and in giving herself for others. Once again she was the messenger of hope and cheery encouragement to one and another in the homes she visited, and many a one looked forward to her coming. But she returned to the empty, poverty-stricken home that was her own, as often as not to find the half-witted husband out and away in his revelling and debauchery. It was then that a great ache came into Sumi's heart and a terrible sense of emptiness and frustration. This continued for some four or five years, with little change either in Sumi San's spiritual condition or any betterment in her material circumstances. She met Mrs. Koide occasionally and was always helped and uplifted by the simple faith of the older woman.

One day Koide San appeared with an invitation to some special meetings. A tent was to be pitched in the neighbourhood and to be the scene of evangelistic endeavour for five days. Would Sumi San come along? There was nothing to detain her at home, for time and again she was alone all evening working or reading and had gone to bed long before her husband returned. The meetings would help to pass the time too, and it was good to be out of doors these hot nights. So she agreed to go along.

The tent was set up on a vacant lot in a busy district and had been furnished with benches made from planks resting on apple boxes. The first night Sumi San slipped in at the back and resisted every effort on the part of the workers to get her to the front. She was quite intrigued with the proceedings, for even if the workers lacked other things they certainly had enthusiasm. The hymns were written on large sheets of paper so that all could read, and were sung with great interest. "What a friend we have in Jesus", "Take the name of Jesus with you" were sung over and over until Sumi San knew them too. The meaning of the words was explained for the benefit of newcomers and illustrated from practical life by the testimonies of some who had already entered this faith. The whole thing had a genuine ring of sincerity to it, and Sumi San was at least impressed.

Then the preacher for the evening mounted the improvised platform, prayed a brief prayer and read his text from the Bible —"For God so loved the world that He gave His only begotten Son that whosoever believeth in Him should not perish but have everlasting life."

He was speaking to newcomers and so would be as simple as possible. The faith that he proclaimed was not some foreign religion as some thought. "The proof of the pudding was in the eating" and they should not reject the message without giving it a hearing. The God mentioned in the text was the God of the whole universe. Just as there was one sun for all countries and one father to each family, so there was one God. He was the Living, Creator God, who loved mankind. It was not to be imagined that the universe came into existence of its own accord, or was fortuitously controlled. Just as everything had a maker, whether the tent he was speaking in or the clothes he was wearing, so the world in the very nature of things demanded a maker. That Maker was God, who also had made man, and who sustained him by His love and care. Man, however, had wandered from God and had wilfully gone into sin; it was for this reason that men's hearts were filled with unrest and dissatisfaction. They were separated by sin from God who wanted to be to them as a father. Only let the problem of sin be settled and man could return to God and in a new unity with Him find salvation from sin and true peace. Was this possible? God had made it possible by the gift of His Only Son Jesus

Christ who died for our sins upon the Cross. He invited any who realised their need of salvation to believe that very evening and to find real peace.

Simply, and in language that all could understand, he preached the Gospel, at times sending the folk into fits of laughter with his apt jokes and at other times having them on the verge of tears with some touching illustration. If the people who attended the first night knew nothing else, they at least understood that God loved and cared for them.

Sumi San went again the second night, and as she left the tent the evangelist spoke to her.

"Honourable wife, you are very welcome. Did you understand tonight?"

"Thank you, I understood a little better tonight."

"Good. Please come again tomorrow, and don't forget— God loves you and wants you to have real peace in your heart."

Sumi San laughed. "If you knew how I have suffered you would not tell me that God loves me. I don't believe in a God of love. Life is a matter of fate and luck. To some the fates are kind and their luck is good. I'm one of the unfortunates. My luck is out and the gods are against me. Good night!"

She went once more during the campaign, but only seemed to be more incensed by what she heard. The best part was the singing of the hymns, which Sumi San greatly loved. As the meetings progressed it was evident that God was working, and numbers raised their hands in token of their making a decision to follow Christ. But Sumi San was not amongst the number.

When the tent had been taken down and sent elsewhere to continue its good work, regular meetings were continued in the church. Numbers had greatly increased as a result of the special meetings, and Pastor Honda was greatly encouraged. Koide San continued tactfully to lead Sumi San into the meetings, and in course of time she became a regular attender at the Sunday gatherings. So the months passed and, though interested, Sumi San was still not definitely committed to the Christian faith.

It must have been about a year after the tent mission when one Sunday evening Pastor Honda "buttonholed" her on the way out of the church.

"Komatsu San, why do you not believe? You came to the tent campaign several times, and I see you in the church every week. Will you not place your faith in Christ who loved you and gave Himself for you?"

Sumi stopped on her way out and replied, "Sensei [Teacher], I will believe if you will show me God. In all the meetings I hear 'God is love, God is love' but no one has showed me Him. When I kneel before the image of Kwannon I feel I have an object for my faith, but here there is nothing to see, "and she waved her hand towards the front of the church. "Show me this God of love and I will believe."

Sumi San was accustomed to using her mind, and she felt that, like other branches of study, faith in Christ was obtained by successful processes of reasoning. However, that evening, in the small vestry off the main church building where Pastor Honda, Koide San and Sumi San talked and prayed, something happened in Sumi's heart that changed her whole course of life.

"The wind bloweth where it listeth and thou hearest the sound thereof, but canst not tell whence it cometh and whither it goeth: so is everyone that is born of the Spirit." We would be labouring in vain if we sought to discover how the mighty miracle of regeneration was wrought in Sumi's heart that night. A much more learned person had asked long ago, 'How can these things be?" and Christ had pointed him to God's gift of His Son. Suffice it to say that the time came that night when reason gave place to faith, and the "why" of the aching heart was fully answered in the simple appropriation of the gift of God in Jesus Christ.

The emotionally sensitive quite possibly and properly experience a sudden and conscious change at conversion. To Sumi the consciousness of the change came slowly, but as day succeeded day the conviction strengthened within her heart that she belonged to Christ. She had committed all to Him, and He in accepting the trust would keep her until that day. Whence came this settled peace in the soul? It was from God! What had rid her heart of the bitterness and hatred towards those who had wronged her? It was God's doing! What had happened that she could look upon that object of revulsion, her profligate, half-wit husband, with love and compassion? It was God's doing! In all the affairs of life, in home and work, in thought and deed, in hope and desire—in all it became indubitably true to Sumi San that "If any man be in Christ he is a new creation; old things have passed away, behold all things have become new." And she rejoiced in it all!

. . . . .

Is any blessing of God imparted without there following a time of testing? It seems not, and Sumi San soon found the circumstances of her daily life becoming increasingly difficult. Happily she could now meet them with the assurance of God's presence and help.

Two years had passed since she was converted when one December morning the whole of Japan was electrified by the news of the war. The Japanese fleet, army and air force had simultaneously launched all-out attacks on Pearl Harbour, Hong Kong and other strong-points in the Pacific area. From then on Japan was committed to all-out war, and soon the people in the home islands were to feel the resultant pinch and pressure. For years the country had been geared to war, but now, already impoverished, still more demands were to be made upon the long-suffering populace. As the war progressed it made itself felt increasingly in the Japanese homeland, and the disturbing air-raids were no doubt unsettling to Jiro's mind, which was already seriously unhinged. The giant B-29 bombers moving up from the South Pacific islands frequently passed over Kobe and Osaka, and the prolonged alerts tried the nerves of even the strongest.

Sumi found that as she moved round on her midwifery visits sometimes Jiro would present himself at the same house in a half-crazed condition, declaring himself to be the midwife's husband. This was, to say the least, embarrassing, and Sumi was perplexed as to the right thing to do. It is the custom in Japan to have a little family celebration on the day the newly-born child is named, and to this the midwife is invited and especially entertained. Jiro San, having noted the houses his wife was visiting in her work, occasionally appeared at these special celebrations and let it be known that he was the husband of Sumi San. The folk of the house could do nothing more than invite him to the feast too, though sometimes they were hard put to it to provide for one, let alone two. At other times he raved up and down the streets in his imbecility and would not be quietened. Only the fact that he was harmless and non-violent prevented his being placed in a mental institution.

The problem was solved in a strange and spectacular way. About this time the planes attacking the Japanese mainland —"B San" as they were familiarly called by the inhabitants—stepped up the number and strength of their sorties as the war entered the year that was to see its end. The alerts were becoming more frequent and of longer duration, and the Japanese were having to spend longer spells in holes, dug-outs and shelters. Then Kobe's turn came, and on the night of the 5th June 1945 the planes swept up and down the narrow coastal plain on which the city is built dropping incendiary and high-explosive bombs. The result was inferno. The lightly built wooden houses burned like matchwood and it seemed impossible that anything in the area could be saved. The people had hastened to places of safety at the alert, and some returning to save their belongings were killed. Sumi San was among the many who lost their homes, though she was able to salvage some personal belongings to enable her to start life over again.

As she stood the next morning and viewed the ruins of her home it became clear to her that there was only one thing to do. She would pack up her few belongings and send them home to Hiroshima Prefecture. There, with her husband, she would stay until the war was over and life returned to normal in a rebuilt Kobe. Within a few days she put her resolve into effect, though not before she had visited the friends at the church. They had all suffered in greater or lesser degree, but it was a strength to Sumi San to see their faith and confidence. "The Lord gave, the Lord has taken away; blessed be the name of the Lord." Many of the Christians were, like herself, preparing to leave for country districts, and it was evident that it would be extremely difficult to continue the regular services in the church.

"Don't forget, Sumi San, that the Lord has said 'I will never leave thee, nor forsake thee', and He will be with you where you go. Give a good testimony and perhaps God will use you to win others to Him in your village. Goodbye and God bless you!"

So said Pastor Honda as she parted from him and the little church which was her soul's birthplace.

The journey to Funo-mura beggars description. After great difficulty Sumi San had been able to forward her luggage. So great was the pressure on the rail system, and so great the confusion caused by the aerial attacks, that no one could tell her when it would arrive. Finally, she and her husband, the latter fortunately in one of his quieter moods, entrained at Sannomiya Station. The coaches were windowless and packed to suffocation, and when the train pulled in people were climbing in and out of the window spaces, not troubling to use the doors. Indeed they could not use them in any case as they were jammed with people. A seat was out of the question, but after long and tiring hours of travel they arrived at length in Hiroshima. There was a long wait before a branch line connection could be made, but in due course they were on their way again. Here the countryside was as it had always been, with no sign at all of the devastation of war. At the end of the rail line they changed and, gathering up their hand luggage, went outside to wait for the bus to take them the last stage of their journey.

"Oi, is this the place?" asked Jiro.

"No, a bit farther. See those mountains over there? Our village lies at the foot of those hills," replied Sumi San.

"What a place! And you expect me to live there?" asked Jiro, although he hardly expected an answer.

After a short time the bus came, but when Sumi San looked round for her husband he was nowhere to be seen. While she had been dozing he had completely disappeared. She tried her best to locate him, but to no avail. And it was alone that Sumi San took up life once more among her beloved mountains.

PART II

THE HAND OF THE MASON

*"I have created him for my glory, I have formed
him; yea, I have made him."*
(Isaiah 43: 7)

Chapter 7

GOD'S WAY IN THE MOUNTAINS

THE casual visitor alighting at Iwami-Oda station would find it very difficult to distinguish it from a hundred other similar stations throughout Japan. As the train enters the station his ear is assailed by a broadcast voice stating that this is without doubt Iwami-Oda and requesting passengers for that station to alight without delay. Across the double tracks the usual kind of footbridge connects the two platforms. Our visitor would pass through the usual kind of exit and find himself outside the station, before which a number of buses are awaiting the time of departure.

Selecting the railway bus which is going to Akana (Red Name), our visitor boards it, and soon after the bus leaves. It makes its way through the crowded streets of the town, skilfully avoiding playing children and parked bicycles, until at length it breaks into the open country with the mountains before it. Leaving the plain with its well-kept fields, the bus heads up the valley, which narrows as the road ascends. By the side of the road the hillside has been terraced wherever possible, and in the small fields so made rice and other crops are grown. But soon the valley becomes so narrow and the sides so steep that even this is impossible. The tree-clad hillsides reach down to the rushing river below, above which, cut out of the solid rock, the road winds up and up and on and on.

At last the summit is reached and from then on the road alternately goes up and down, passing through isolated villages until at length it comes into the Go River valley at Kasubuchi. Here it connects with a branch railway line that has come up the wide river valley from the coast. Our visitor, however, has still farther to go. His destination is Sawadani—Marsh Valley— which lies ahead another five or six miles. As he leaves the country town, and with it the railway, he catches a glimpse of the dam which has recently been thrown across the Go River for the purpose of generating electricity. The bus now turns

59

away up a tributary of the main river, and once again the road follows the winding river up and up towards its source. On either side the trees are beautiful indeed, outstanding among them the cypress and pine, the fir and the oak, while huddled around their feet are all kinds of scrub undergrowth.

The bus stops and our visitor alights in Sawadani village. The village is in fact a group of hamlets scattered here and there along the road, and up in the mountains, for a distance of some eight or nine miles. Altogether there are some four hundred houses and living in them a population of some two thousand people. The villagers make their living by farming and lumbering. The farms are small and the paddy-fields largely terraced, and owing to the mountainous nature of the terrain the growing season is short. To supplement their income the farmers breed silkworms, which three times in the year are hatched out and cared for until they go up into their cocoons. Others haul the lumber from the hillsides down to the road in the valley, while still others cut and burn the scrubby bushes and small trees for charcoal. All in all, money is none too plentiful in the village.

With the coming of December winter begins to close in on the villagers and after the New Year the snow falls in real earnest. Two or three feet of snow is common, and for the long weeks of winter there is little the farmers can do. The farms cannot support more than one family, so as the children grow older all except the eldest son move out to the wider world beyond the village. Some go to work in the mines farther west in Yamaguchi Prefecture, others seek employment in the larger towns on the coast, while the girls go off to work in spinning mills in the bigger cities. Sawadani is in effect like an incubator—the young are reared there only to find their ultimate destination in places far removed from their birthplace.

Were we to follow the bus still farther on its climb through the mountains we would at length come to Akana, the terminus. There we could catch a second bus which would take us over the border into Hiroshima Prefecture and the village where Sumi San had once more taken up residence.

.   .   .   .   .

It was a late summer day in 1945 in Sawadani village. The sky was a wonderful arch of blue over the tree-covered hillsides that enclose the narrow valley. It was early yet for the autumn colours to appear, but up on the mountain the trunks of the cryptomeria trees glowed a dull red in the warm light of the sunshine. A solitary kite wheeled and wheeled again, occasionally uttering its shrill, piping call. Along the roadside the rice plants stood up fine and firm, with just the suspicion of the coming transformation into gold that harvest time would bring. The farmers were happy, the dreaded 210th day and 220th day had passed without wind and storm, the flowers had "set" and the rice was already forming in the ears. Typhoon or storm in September can in a day wreck and ruin the farmers' crop of rice and deprive them of their staff of life.

Outside the village office in Kokonoka, one of the hamlets in Sawadani, a solitary woman sat on a stone in the shade by the bus stop. It was Sumi San. A middle-aged man came out of the office and paused to say:

"Good day. It is still very hot, isn't it?"

"Yes, indeed; but how good it is to have the fine weather."

"Ah, what you say is only too true. The farmers hereabouts are so glad that the 210th day passed without a storm. Now if we can avoid rain-storms until harvest we shall be all right. It looks as though there will be a bumper crop this year."

"Is that so? No doubt it is the goodness of God."

"Quite right, the gods are good to us." Sumi San's emphasis was different, but her words in Japanese could be construed in a very general way, and this the villager unconsciously did! The man continued:

"You are a stranger here?"

"Yes, this is the first time I have been in Sawadani, though I am a near neighbour. My home is over the hills there in Funo village, Hiroshima Prefecture," and Sumi San pointed to the ridge of high hills at the head of the valley.

"Is that so? So near and yet so far. As the bird flies it is near, but as the bus crawls it is indeed far distant."

"Yes, and now I am awaiting the bus to return."

"You have finished your business here?"

"Why, yes! As a matter of fact I came to look for some luggage of mine, but without success."

"That is too bad. But, if it is not rude, tell me how your luggage came to be lost."

"It is a long story, so please sit down," and Sumi San rose from her seat on the stone. Then she told him of being bombed out in Kobe, and of sending her baggage ahead before she journeyed home to Funo village.

"They could not trace the baggage at our nearest railway station, so wondered if it had travelled along the San-in line instead of the San-yo line. You know the characters are very alike?"

The man nodded in agreement.

"So the railway authorities phoned to Kasubuchi station down the hill here, and right enough there were some unidentified goods there. So today I came over by bus to see the goods, but found they were not mine. Then I was directed here to Sawadani as someone here had received luggage in error, but again the bags were not mine. So I'm afraid my journey has been a fruitless one."

"Well, that certainly is too bad. I hope the baggage turns up in due course." Then after a pause the villager continued, "Are you working in Funo village?"

"No, at the moment I am doing nothing. You see, I am a nurse and there is already one in our village, so I am not needed there."

"A nurse, eh? We are in need of a welfare nurse here: would you care to come over and help us? You know how with the war on so many nurses have been drafted to army hospitals. If you would consider coming, I will gladly mention it to the village head."

"That is very kind of you. I should need to think the matter over a little and you would of course want to see my references and examine my qualifications."

"Yes, of course! But still there would be no harm in mentioning it to the village head, would there?"

"No, I should be glad if you would do that, and then if you would let me know the result I could come over for an interview."

"That's right. Would you let me have your address, and then I can get in touch with you," concluded the villager.

Sumi San complied with the request, wondering at the same time if God was in this unexpected encounter. They chatted together a little longer, and when the bus came Sumi San boarded it and was soon on her way home.

We need not trace the subsequent events in detail. Suffice it to say that conditions on both sides were acceptable, and within two or three weeks Sumi San had moved over the mountain divide into Sawadani village to become the health visitor and midwife for the district. Accommodation was found for her in the upstairs of a house just near the village office, and there she made her abode. God had certainly guided her. "I being in the way the Lord led me" had been true, and the luggage lost in transit had been the means of bringing her to what proved to be a fruitful field of service for God.

.   .   .   .   .

"Honourable wife, is the pain very bad?"

"It is sharp, but I can bear it, if only the gods give me this child."

"You have no other children, honourable wife?"

"No! Three times have I hoped, but each time the little one has died; and now if no child is born the husband will send me away in shame. What good indeed is a wife that cannot bear children?"

"But you are strong and well, honourable wife. This time the child will be given."

"I have done all I can. Twice weekly for the last year I have worshipped at the Hachiman Shrine and given much money. I have visited the Hitomaru Shrine in Totsuga village and worshipped there. And see, round my neck I have this charm, which is said to assure the birth of a child. I have done all I can, the gods will surely hear me."

"Honourable wife, I have no children myself, but I am not in despair. My faith is in the Living God, in Jesus Christ, and I know He answers prayer."

"Ah, what name was that, nurse?"

"Jesus Christ. I have trusted in Him for many years. Shall I pray to Him for you?"

"I have heard the name. It is a foreign name, a Western god, and we are Japanese. I doubt if He can help me, but it can do no harm. But can you pray who are not a priest?"

"Yes, if our hearts are true and sincere the most unlearned can pray and be heard. Let us close our eyes and pray, honourable wife."

The single dim lamp lighted the scene as the Christian nurse prayed for the farmer's wife. The room was so blackened with the smoke of years that the walls reflected scarcely any light. The smell of stale smoke from the open stove, standing on the earthen floor, mingled with that of the grass mats that constituted the raised floor of the living-room. The wife lay in thick padded quilts, breathing heavily, irregularly, with a look of fear and apprehension in her dark eyes. There was another Presence there too, unseen, yet real, as the nurse poured out her heart to God, the Living God, for her patient. Behind, the candles glimmered before the Buddhist shrine, indistinctly revealing the offerings of tea and rice newly placed there at nightfall.

"Thank you, nurse. You think He heard? It was a lovely prayer, and you spoke as if He were here."

"He is here, honourable wife. And I'm sure He heard, but we can only leave everything to Jesus. He will do what is best."

"Ah, but it must be a child! I must give my husband a son. If I fail this time I must go home—empty, ashamed."

"Now, now! Just rest quietly. It will be a while yet, so I will come again. The Living God He can give life."

Sumi San went out into the night. It was her first winter in Sawadani and the snow was piled up to a depth of three to four feet. She pulled her cape more tightly round her and settled her wide-brimmed *kasa* or straw hat more firmly on her head. The road was quite blocked by the snow, and a narrow gully in it had been made by the feet of the few who had passed that way. As she trudged along she prayed for the wife she had left, that God would indeed give her the child and open her heart to the Saviour.

It was just getting light when she went out again. More snow had fallen while she rested and it was heavy going on foot. She plodded bravely on and after a short while reached the farmhouse that was her destination. All had been proceeding normally, and by the time the sun had tinted with pink the snow-decorated firs on the hillside a bonny little boy had been born into the family. The woman's joy knew no bounds, and Sumi San had difficulty in restraining her enthusiasm in her weakened condition. Days later, when she was up and about and the baby was thriving, nothing would do but she must make an offering to this Christ. A few flowers perhaps, or some rice cakes, or would a gift of money be suitable? Where should she take the offering, was there a shrine somewhere near? Just as resolutely Sumi San told her that God did not expect her offerings and there was no shrine nearby, for God did not dwell in temples made by man. The woman finally overcame the problem by giving a gift to the nurse who had delivered her child by the help of Jesus Christ.

Thus Sumi San worked, both as a nurse and a midwife, up and down the village. There was only one doctor in the whole general area and he would attend only to those who came to his clinic. He refused to make professional calls. So it was to the nurse that the people came, and it was she who dressed their cuts and sores and gave them injections. Even a patient down with 'flu, as common in Japan as in the West, was not beyond the reach of her care. She would travel off the main road up and up into the narrowing valley to visit such a patient in an isolated farmhouse. Nothing was too much bother. In the heat of summer and the cold of winter, through rain and shine she went like a ministering angel from house to house. And not only did she attend to physical needs, she always had a word of cheer and encouragement, and not infrequently prayed for her patients. No wonder that the villagers spoke appreciatively of the new health visitor to one another, saying, as they had said of her Master, "What manner of person is this?"

Not the least of the things that impressed the village folk was the nurse's attitude to money. Quite often the villagers had little ready cash and were unable at once to pay the midwife for her services. In deserving cases she refused to take anything at all and was always ready to wait if there was temporary hardship. At best her remuneration was small, and Sumi San lived a life of genuine sacrifice to help the village people. Distances were great, but for a long time she would buy no bicycle. Pulling on the loose trousers or *mompei* which the farmer women use, and shouldering her rucksack, she would trudge all over her "parish" ministering to the needy.

As she worked away in her professional capacity one thing greatly saddened Sumi San—the prevalence of immorality in the village. Not infrequently she was called to help in the birth of illegitimate children, and the village folk seemed to treat the matter as a more or less formal thing. The child was soon absorbed into the mother's family and no questions were asked.

In spring and autumn heathen festivals were held in the village, and at such times the young people would put on amateur theatricals. For weeks before the festival practices were held, often lasting quite late into the night. Then the young people would disperse, to travel together the dark and lonely roads to their homes. Or, as was sometimes the case, they would stay overnight in the place where the practice had taken place, with inevitable consequences. The moral conscience of the villagers was far from being sensitive. The winter days were long and entertainments in the village were few. Apart from an occasional travelling film show, Kasubuchi had the nearest movie theatre, and who could travel so far in the snow? So the young people were largely excused their indiscretions.

Sumi San was burdened in her heart and wanted to do something about this sad state of affairs. She had not felt free to propagate the Gospel openly—one had to move slowly in the rural districts—so that her chief recourse was to prayer. And pray she did, continually and fervently.

Chapter 8

THE MASTER PLAN REVEALED

"OI, d'you hear that? She's at it again."

The housewife listened carefully with her husband to the muttered voice or voices coming from the room above them.

"Yes, I hear it all right and I don't like it. There's something uncanny about this nurse, muttering away there night after night."

"You don't suppose there's anybody up there with her, do you? Sometimes I think I hear two voices."

"How could that be, honourable father? We should soon know if anyone came into the house. A person couldn't get up any other way, could they?"

"Well, there is that old shed out at the back, and if anybody wanted they could climb the persimmon tree on to the roof and get in that way. Still, I don't think the nurse is the kind of person to entertain men in her own room."

"Honourable father, I was talking to Mrs. Takahashi the other day. You know her daughter-in-law is expecting a little one sometime and the nurse is attending her. She told me that whenever the neighbours meet the nurse on the road, especially at night time, she is always muttering away to herself. Indeed Mrs. Takahashi says they would change to another midwife if there were one, but there's no one else in the village."

"Hmm. She's still at it. D'you know, wife, I believe she's possessed of a spirit, perhaps of the Fox-god, Inari San. I've heard that when people have an evil spirit in them they mutter away to themselves like someone half crazy. Yes, that's what it is, she's possessed by an evil spirit, and I'm afraid this is going to bring bad luck on our house. We can't tolerate that. We may have the judgment of the gods on our home and crops. Wife, there's only one thing—she must leave."

"Yes; but, honourable father, we were specially asked by the village office to put her up. How can we turn her out?"

"I'll fix that. I'll see someone in the office and get that problem solved. I just can't stand this mutter, mutter all evening and each evening. It'll drive me crazy too, and besides we'll have bad luck."

"Well, whatever you say. There's certainly something strange about the nurse."

A few days later Sumi San was called into the village office, and there the official specially concerned with her branch of the work said:

"Nurse, I'm afraid we'll have to find some fresh rooms for you. The people you're staying with have a married son coming home and they need the accommodation upstairs."

"Is that so? That is too bad, as the house is quite central in the village."

"Yes, but it can't be helped. Would you like to find your own place, as you are better acquainted with the village now, or shall we find lodgings for you?"

"Thank you, I think I can find somewhere. I'm on the move all the time and can enquire about new rooms."

"Too bad, nurse, to put this added burden on you," concluded the official.

"Not at all, I can find a corner somewhere," replied Sumi San as she left the office. And so a move was made, but it was not until long months afterwards that the nurse learned the true reason for her having to leave her rooms. Nor, indeed, was that the end, for once again she had to move. Possibly if she had mentioned that she was a Christian and that she was simply spending her spare time in prayer the folk would have understood. It was because the burden of the souls in Sawadani weighed so heavily upon her that she was continually praying, even when walking along the country roads. She was praying in secret, convinced that her Heavenly Father would reward her openly. And in the dispensation of God the time was drawing near when in Sawadani the glorious Gospel of the Living God would be proclaimed.

But we must retrace our steps a little.

.   .   .   .   .

It was some twelve to fifteen years before the point we have reached in our story when one evening, just as the sun was casting long shadows across Chihara in Sawadani village, a villager opened the door in Mrs. Takahashi's house and called out a friendly "Good evening".

"Ah, Noguchi San, is it? Maa, please rest a while."

"Thank you, honourable wife, but is your husband in?"

"Yes, he's out at the back, just in from the fields. I'll call him," and she went through to the rear of the house. After a few moments they reappeared, Mrs. Takahashi's man dressed in clothes stained with the soil of honest toil and with rubber-soled *tabi* (a kind of sock) on his feet.

"Fine weather, Noguchi San. Just right for the crops."

"Indeed truly so, Takahashi San. I'm sorry to trouble you when you are tired, but my husband asked me to come over. A short while ago a young fellow called at our house and asked if he could stay the night. He comes from over the border in Hiroshima Prefecture and cannot get back tonight, and of course there are no inns in our village. We don't like accommodating strangers, but he seems a genuine fellow and we would put him up, only our house is full just now. My daughter has just come back for a while with her two children and we are just full up, and indeed we haven't enough quilts for any more. So my man wondered if you could put him up just for tonight."

"Hmm, I wonder," said Takahashi, thinking. Then more briskly, "What do you think, wife?"

"Well, if he seems a reliable fellow we could do it. What is he here for?"

"He says he is after a job at the village office and came over to make enquiries. Certainly he seems more of the educated type."

"If that is so, then it should be safe enough to put him up. What do you say, father?"

"Yes, Noguchi San, we'll do it. Send him round."

"We'll give him his evening meal and then after that I'll come round with him. Sorry to have troubled you!"

The young fellow came to the Takahashis' house that night and was there for many a month afterwards, for he was given the job at the village office and found his first resting-place in Sawadani a permanent home.

As Mrs. Noguchi had said, he was certainly of the studious type and he had quite a small library in his room. Sometimes when he was out Mrs. Takahashi would glance at the books, and many of them seemed to be about Christianity. There was a black-covered book with gilt edges bearing the title "Old and New Covenant Holy Book", which she was later to learn was the Bible. She wondered why he, a Japanese, should bother with such a foreign religion, but then he was a student and probably studied it for interest. At the village office he was known as a reliable worker and a steady youth. In the house he kept pretty much to himself and spent a good part of his evenings in his room. He was not physically strong and probably felt he had to rest as much as possible. No one knew much about his relatives, and with Japanese discreetness none asked any questions.

Then one day a message came for him to return to his home in Hiroshima Prefecture owing to illness there, and he went, never to return. Sometime later a message came to say he was himself ill, and sometime later still came news of his death. Months passed into years and no one came to claim his belongings, and at length the Takahashis sold them for what they would fetch. The Christian books went with the rest and the episode was closed. Yet in the wonderful purposes of God the prayers of that unnamed young man did not fall to the ground. The coming of Sumi San was one answer, and what later transpired was a much fuller answer to yet another who had prayed to His Heavenly Father in secret.

.　　.　　.　　.　　.

After two or three changes Sumi San found a more or less permanent lodging place in Chihara, which was farther down the valley from the village office and her previous home.

Travelling by bus to Sawadani from the railway line that hugs the coast, one comes first of all to Chihara. There some seven or eight houses facing a similar number on the other side of the road give the appearance of solidity to the otherwise scattered community. A little beyond the bus-stop a road from a branch valley joins the main road, and running up the side road from the corner were a few more houses and shops. It was in the corner house that Sumi San was able to find accommodation. The owner was a former schoolteacher who was also in charge of one of the local Shinto shrines. In the lower part of the main house he had started a shop, but the annexe of the building, consisting of two six-mat rooms (roughly nine feet by twelve each), was vacant. There was a separate entrance into the annexe, and Sumi San viewed this with satisfaction, for she anticipated starting meetings as soon as possible. A more central place in so scattered an area it would have been difficult to find. To complete the picture, just a little farther up the road a laughing, bubbling stream ran parallel with the side road behind the shops and houses, as it hurried to join the main tributary on its way down to the Go River.

And now, after having lived in Sawadani for three years, Sumi San had the growing conviction that God was leading her to preach Christ there. Yet what could she, a poor weak woman, do? Prayer was still her main weapon, and she had recourse to it again and again. Gradually the plan began to take shape. We have spoken before of Sumi's frugality and thrift. In spite of the general poverty of the village and the smallness of the remuneration she received, she had managed to save the sum of three to four thousand yen. This represented possibly a little less than would come into her hands in the course of a month's work as health visitor. She felt that even the fact she had saved that amount was due to the kindness of the villagers, and at one time she thought of donating it to the village for some good cause or other. But wait, was there not a better use to which it could be allocated?

The burden of the immorality of the village was upon her heart, and she longed to tell them of the victorious power that is in Christ! Yes, she would give the village a lasting gift, the gift of the Gospel. She would use the money for evangelistic effort and pray that God would purify the village community where she had found a home.

.   .   .   .   .

The year was 1948. Three years had passed since the end of the war, and conditions in bomb-blasted Japan were only slowly improving. Little by little the cities that had been razed to the ground were taking shape again, but communications were far from normal. Trains were few and terribly crowded, and in the cities the street-cars still had no seats. Food was scarce too, and the prunes and corn-meal which the occupation forces rationed out were new to the Japanese. They did not know how to use them. The occupation forces themselves were in all parts of Japan, though the country area around which our story centres saw nothing of them. Indeed the results of war that were visible were few—chiefly those silent white marker posts outside the village homes which told of some loved one lost in battle. Throughout Japan in the wake of defeat had come a tremendous interest in Christianity. General Douglas McArthur had given every encouragement to missionaries to return to the country, and Japanese pastors were constantly busy preaching Christ here and there. Among them was Pastor Honda of Mikage, though he was no longer in charge of the church there. A bigger vision and burden was his. In downtown Kobe, near the Fukuhara red-light district which Jira had frequented, the Gospel Hall had been burned to the ground and its witness silenced. It grieved Honda San that the witness was silenced in the hall he knew so well as a student, and he began to pray and plan. At last he managed to borrow a tent of sorts, so old that when it rained it was necessary to use umbrellas inside(!), and there he began to preach Christ on the site of the former Gospel Hall. Hundreds came, hundreds heard and many believed. Honda San gathered in all the help he could and speedily pressed the believers into service.

One day to the pastor's poor shack of a home there came a letter from Sumi San. Could he possibly come to Sawadani and conduct evangelistic meetings? And she outlined her concern and burden. How he would like to have gone to help this lone witness, one of his own spiritual children, yet how could he leave the important and growing work on the old Mission Hall site? He replied explaining his position and suggesting the nurse wrote to Hashimoto Sensei, whom she also knew from Mikage days.

A second letter was despatched and this found its way into the home of Pastor Hashimoto.

Dear Pastor Hashimoto,

Praise the Name of the Lord Jesus! At last the cold snows of winter are retreating, and soon the new growth of spring will appear. I trust that in the goodness of God both you, Sensei, and your family are well and that you are being much used of the Lord. These are difficult days, but God is blessing our country and many are seeking the Saviour.

I am writing to you about this village of Sawadani where I am living. It is a very scattered mountain village, with small fields and poor houses. Moreover, it is extremely immoral and its people greatly need the Gospel of Christ. I cannot give you a big thank-offering, but if you come I will pay your expenses. Do please come and make five believers here. I am the only Christian and have no one to share the burden of this village. Please come and preach Christ so that prayer-fellows may be given to me. If you can come in March, when the deep snow has gone and the farmers are not yet busy, that will be the best time.

Please take care of yourself and excuse my untidy characters.

With this request I sign myself,
KOMATSU SUMI.

The pastor recalled the writer, for he had frequently met Sumi San when he attended Mikage Church while still a student in Bible School. He was, however, surprised to get the letter. She had never been what one might call an outstanding Christian, almost on the slow side in things spiritual. Yet here she was actually planning an evangelistic effort in her own village.

Mr. Hashimoto's first impulse was to turn down the invitation. For one thing he was tired out and none too well. But recently he had been conducting evangelistic meetings amid the deep snow of north Japan in the Buddhist stronghold of Niigata. Added to that he was suffering from inflammation of the ear occasioned by a dowsing in a cold river at Harima Shingu. His lodgings there were separated from the meeting place by a broad but shallow stream and he had to cross it once or twice daily. Heavy rain had swollen the river considerably and the current was swift when, at the end of the afternoon meeting one day, his hostess had offered to punt him across to the home side. The tide-rip, however, was more than even the housewife had imagined, and soon the boat was heading towards the weir with nothing between them and danger but the safety wire stretched tautly between the two banks. Up went the pole as they swept under the wire, but it failed to halt the progress of the boat. The pastor grabbed the wire and was stopped dead while the boat went on, to be pulled safely ashore a little lower down. But Hashimoto San suffered an unseasonable bath in the cold river, with the unpleasant result we have already noted.

The invitation from Sawadani was, however, so pressing that he felt he should go, though he wondered how many people would gather in such a lonely and scattered area. Then he recalled the interest of Mrs. Koide in Sumi San in the days before Kobe was bombed, and extended an invitation to both husband and wife to accompany him. At length plans were complete. The meetings were to begin on the 18th March in the house at the parting of the ways in Chihara. Sumi San was overjoyed at the prospect, and day and night the burden of her prayers was for five fellow Christians to be given her in the village.

Chapter 9

THE BUILDING TAKES SHAPE

THE bus stopped at the appointed place in Chihara and out stepped Pastor Hashimoto.

"Ah, Sensei, you have come so long a distance, you must be tired. And Koide San! Why, this is grand! How long it is since I saw you. I trust you are honourably well?"

Sumi San fairly bubbled over with joy as she greeted the visitors upon whom, under God, she set such great hopes.

"This way, please. Let me have that bag. No, it's not too heavy. Just up the road here a few metres."

She walked ahead and soon all were sitting around the fire bowl in her home, sipping green tea. The snow indeed had gone, but it was quite cold still.

"Is this where we are to have the meetings?" asked the pastor.

"Yes, we have twelve mats here for the regular services, and I have also rented the upstairs for prayer and personal work." Then in a whisper, "The owner is the priest at the local shrine, but having been a schoolteacher for years is quite enlightened." Sumi San laughed. "He is not at all opposed to having the meetings."

"But, Komatsu San, this is a very scattered area and the nights are dark. Do you think the people will come?" asked the pastor doubtfully.

"Yes, I believe they will come. I have prayed much, told many people about the meetings, and have also stuck up a few posters here and there through the district."

"Fine. Let's keep believing. Could we have some prayer now?"

Forthwith the little group bowed their heads and hearts to the God who is not willing that any should perish, and implored Him to save souls in Sawadani village.

It was seven o'clock the same evening when Pastor Hashimoto rose to his feet to open the first meeting. Even the most optimistic hopes had been exceeded and the twelve-mat room was filled to capacity with some forty or so people. He stood at a small table and behind him pinned on the wall was a large sheet of paper with the words of the hymn "O Wanderer return" written in large Japanese characters.

"We are now going to commence the first Christian meeting in Sawadani village. Many of you will know little more of Christianity than the name, and will think that it is a foreign religion of no interest to us Japanese. The reason these meetings have been convened is to give you all at least an opportunity of hearing the Gospel. For four nights we shall be speaking here of God and sin, of peace and joy, of this life and the world to come, and we want you to listen carefully. In Christian meetings we always sing, and here we have a hymn that has by popular selection been proved to be the best-loved in Japan. I'll sing the first verse to you and then please all join in without any reserve. It doesn't matter if you make a mistake, and you'll soon pick up the tune."

With these opening remarks the pastor launched into the hymn, and after several tries he had the younger part of his audience singing, even if the older people remained stolid and unmoved. The folk began to feel more at ease as an occasional and timely joke broke down natural reserve. The workers were conscious in an unusual way of the presence of God, and the power of the Lord was present to heal. Prayer briefly and simply uttered preceded further singing of the same hymn and an explanation of its meaning. Mr. Koide told of what Christ had done for him in practical and easy-to-be-understood phrases. And now at last the message was given—the first time as far as is known that Christ had been publicly proclaimed as a Saviour from sin in that community.

We will not follow the message in detail. From things that were known the pastor led them to the hidden truths of the Gospel; from things that were old he led them to facts that were new. His listeners forgot their previous prejudice against "Yasu-kyo" as an imported faith and found that what was preached came very near home indeed. This was certainly not error, not a misguided belief; this was practical, what the pastor said was right. And as later on they passed out into the night they were saying one to another "*Yokatta*, it was good! It was good!"

As the farmers were more or less at leisure in the month of March, afternoon meetings had been arranged also, and the next day at two o'clock found a goodly company present. To the pastor's great joy many of them were there for the second time. There was not quite the same freedom in the meeting as on the previous night, but the pastor put it down to his own personal tiredness. Certainly the people listened well, were very friendly, and one or two of the men even stayed behind to ask questions. The meeting over, Sumi San, Mr. and Mrs. Koide and the pastor sat around sipping tea and discussing the progress of the Gospel.

"There'll be more out tonight, Pastor, for some are busy during the day. It is fine to see the same people coming too," remarked Sumi San.

"Yes, it was good to see those middle-aged women there," returned the pastor. "Do you know them?"

"Why, yes, I have been in the homes of most of them helping to bring their little ones into the world." Sumi San stopped and looked anxiously at Pastor Hashimoto, then said excitedly, "Pastor, are you feeling rather unwell? Koide San, quick. . .!"

But before anyone could reach him the cup of tea had dropped from his hand and Pastor Hashimoto had rolled over on the floor and lay there unconscious. Quickly Mr. and Mrs. Koide went into action, loosening the pastor's collar and applying wet cloths to his forehead, and in a short while he had recovered consciousness. It was obvious that he was far from well, so the quilts were spread out on the floor and he was persuaded to rest for a while. The accumulated tiredness and fatigue resulting from the meetings in Niigata and Shingu, together with the after-effects of the fall into the river at the latter place, were taking their toll. This was not just a fainting fit but something in the nature of a slight stroke. It was obviously doubtful if the pastor would be able to continue the meetings. Perhaps the most agitated of all was Sumi San. When Hashimoto San had recovered somewhat, she was down at his side saying:

"Pastor, you must get better quickly. God has sent you to this place especially to open it up to the Gospel. If we have to stop the meetings now because of your illness, these superstitious village folk will be sure to say that the judgment of the gods has fallen on you, and that Christianity is a false religion. Bear up, Pastor; be brave and God will see you through. He will not let His great Name be dishonoured. Here, eat these pickled plums," and she produced some sour plums, which in the eyes of the Japanese have great medicinal properties. "We will pray for you, we will hold up your hands as did Aaron and Hur the arms of Moses. I believe! I believe! Koide San, let us pray for the pastor."

United prayer was offered to the life-giving God, and as they prayed the pastor was wonderfully strengthened and into his own heart came the assurance that he should preach that evening and that God would see him through.

The rooms were packed again that night as the pastor rose to speak. He told afterwards how that he felt dizzy all the time and gripped the little table before him to prevent himself from swaying from side to side. Behind him were two Scripture texts written on long strips of paper hanging between the ceiling and the floor. One declared that "The wages of sin is death", but the other proclaimed that "The gift of God is eternal life through Jesus Christ". The word of God pierced and searched into the inner recesses of the hearts of the hearers. The devil had been defeated in his attempt to silence the Gospel, and the pastor was able to complete the series of meetings without further infirmity.

By the third day souls were getting desperate about their sin. Sumi San had anticipated this and the necessity of the pastor being able to do personal work quietly. For this purpose she had rented the upstairs portion of the house, which ran over her living-rooms a little to the back. When some of the younger folk asked to talk with the pastor she directed them to the upstair room, and there real transactions with God were undertaken. In the quiet of the upper room, away from the merely curious, seeking souls were able to pour out their hearts before God. The pastor lent a sympathetic ear as they told of their faults and failure, of sin and defeat, and pointed them to the Lamb of God which beareth away the sin of the world. One young woman was so anxious to clear up the past that she brought along her diary and with its aid made a thorough-going confession to God. The more solid the foundation the more sure the building. It was the house built upon the rock that stood firm. We live in days of "easy-believism", with the result that our lands are peopled with mere professors. One of the main reasons for the solid work done at this time in Sawadani was the honest and realistic dealing with sin. The ground of the soul was cleared, thoroughly cleared by wholesome confession and honest repentance, and upon the cleansed site was built the structure of a new man in Christ.

Into the enquiry room upstairs there came one evening young Takahashi. From the first he had come to the meetings and felt the tug of the Holy Spirit at his heart. He would not have explained it that way, indeed the terms would have been foreign to him; but he sensed the need of deliverance from sin and defeat that dogged his life. He longed for the assurance of peace and victory that he had learned Christ could give, and he found it that night. He was followed by his younger brother and his sister, and who can doubt that their salvation was in answer to prayer. Many years before the young fellow employed at the village office had lived in their home and prayed, and now at length it seemed as if his prayers were answered for the Takahashi family at least.

And the work was not limited to Chihara. Taking advantage of the fact that the farmers were not too busy, it was possible to arrange a meeting in Kokonoka-ichi—or Ninth Day Market. This was farther up the valley and near the village office where Sumi San had first been invited to serve as health visitor in the district. It was an afternoon meeting but the workers were encouraged to see a good crowd gathered, and one very representative of the hamlet as a whole, for both young and old were there. There was Mr. Nitta and his wife. He was a stone-mason and almost as silent as the stone he fashioned. Whether his heart was as hard and impervious to the voice of God we do not know, but God worked in both him and his wife from that day on to will and to do of His good pleasure.

In the nearest railway town of Kasubuchi a Christian woman came to light. News had reached her of the Christian meetings in Sawadani and revived in her heart an interest that had been dormant for a few years. She had been led to Christ in Kobe, but had been bombed out of the city and, like Sumi San, had returned to her native place to live. So a warm invitation was extended to Mr. Hashimoto and his party to visit the town and have meetings there, and this he was able to do. The result was that regular meetings were started in the town, although they

ceased a few years later when the Christian woman had to move
to another town.

Space does not permit us to follow in detail the day-by-day
progress of the meetings. At the end of the scheduled four
days it was evident that a number had made definite commit-
ments to Christ. Sumi San was overjoyed.

"Pastor, what a wonderful work you have done!"

"No, Komatsu San, it is not I but God who has done the
work in answer to your prayers and faithful witness."

"Pastor, I asked you to come for four days; but the response
is so good, will you please stay for another two days? I have
saved up a little money and I will give you a bigger thank-
offering if you will stay."

"Komatsu San, that is very kind of you, but I did not come
for what I could get out of the meetings, I came to give the
Gospel of the grace of God to those who have never heard it."

"I realise that, but you have given of your valuable time and
have to live too. I have actually saved up about three thousand yen, and that will pay your fare and that of Mr. and Mrs.
Koide and leave a little over for a gift. I would like to do more
than that, but I cannot. That is all I have. But you will stay for
another two days?"

"Certainly. I'll be glad to, for it so happens that I have no
other responsibilities for the next few days."

So the pastor and his two friends stayed on, and finally, after
some six days, reluctantly but positively had to leave. Before
he went, however, Sumi San and her visitors assessed as best
they could what had been done during the period. The pastor
had taken some twenty-four meetings in various places and
about twenty-seven souls had professed faith in Christ. Sumi
San was torn between joy and perplexity.

"Pastor, when I wrote to you I asked you to make me five
prayer-fellows here in Sawadani, and you have made twenty-
seven. What can I do now? I cannot preach, and in any case it
is hardly a woman's work; and yet we cannot leave these souls
alone, we must have meetings for them. How can I lead them
on?"

"That is a difficulty, but the best thing you can do is to have
a little Bible Study meeting each week. Gather the enquirers
together and sing the hymns we have been singing in the
special meetings. Then read the Bible to them and get them

to buy Bibles and read them too. You must give your testimony, telling them what God has done for you and how He has led you. Then you can pray with them and teach them to pray too. God will help you, for the Holy Spirit is our Teacher. And remember, 'God hath chosen the weak things of the earth to confound the mighty.' "

"Well, we'll do that. As I said, I can't preach, but we will meet each Saturday evening."

The pastor and Mr. and Mrs. Koide left, but somehow Sumi San did not feel lonely. She already felt that she had new friends in Sawadani, and that among the twenty or more who had professed there were those who would be real prayer-fellows with her in the coming days. But, wait, would the people come to the regular Saturday meetings? It was one thing to come out to the special meetings to hear a visiting speaker from the city, but would those who had professed be willing to face the ostracism and approbrium of the village folk and stand out for Christ? Sumi San need have had no fears. In that little upper room so honest had been the confession and repentance, and so thorough the work of the Holy Spirit, that the people came and continued to come. Some gave evidence of being truly born again from that time onwards, and their faith increased from strength to strength. It was noticed too that these were the very ones who had made a clean break with the old past life. Those who had not entered the enquiry room and there had definite transactions with God came for a while but then quietly slipped away and came no more.

The hand of the Master Mason was at work fashioning living stones for His Temple from the rough material of Sawadani.

Chapter 10

WEATHERED BY THE STORM

WITH the coming of the month of May, Pastor Hashimoto was once again in Sawadani. There is possibly no relationship so strong as that between parent and child, and he was anxious to return to see how his children in the faith were progressing. The over-all picture was good. Most of those who had professed the name of Christ in March had come through into a real experience of conversion. Among them several young men of the village were full of promise and were proving a real strength to Komatsu San. The Takahashi brothers were developing well and seemed to have the gift of leadership. Watanabe San, a farmer in Chihara, was also attending regularly and showing signs of real spiritual life, and being an older man he helped to give stability to the little group. And already the village in general was being impressed by the earnestness of the young people and the evident change in their lives.

It would be surprising indeed if such an outstanding advance into the territory of the enemy of souls could be carried out without opposition of some kind or another, and soon this became apparent. One afternoon, during the meetings conducted by him in May, a visitor came to see Pastor Hashimoto. He was on the young side of forty and neatly dressed in Western clothes. The pastor was quite frankly surprised to see a person of this type in such a remote country village and puzzled in his mind as to who his guest might be. After the usual greetings the pastor said, "Have you been attending the meetings here?" to which the visitor replied in the affirmative. The pastor could not recall having seen him, but that could easily be explained. He had most probably been wearing the loose-fitting Japanese kimono, which was in general use and which would render him quite inconspicuous in the crowd; and as every preacher knows, some people seem to impress themselves upon one's memory from the first, while others can go in

and out of the same gathering without being particularly
noticed. Thus to the pastor the visitor was quite a stranger.

"I have come along to ask you a few questions, if I may
trespass upon your time," said the visitor.

"You are very welcome indeed. I am just holding meetings
in the evenings, so through the day am glad to speak to any
who are interested in Christianity. Have you any special
problems? What do you think of the teaching you have
heard?"

"Well, what I have heard so far I feel to be in general good,
but various problems have been raised in my mind. For example, in Buddhism the object of faith and worship is before
our eyes. We bow our heads before the *butsudan* [the Buddhist
family altar], or before a stone Jizo San, or an image of Kwannon, and sense as we pray and worship that we are in touch
with the spirit of the being we are worshipping. Now do you
have anything like that in Christianity? Can you say to me,
'Here, worship this'? If you have no definite object of worship
which is concrete and visible, how can you know that you are in
touch with God, and that He answers prayer as you say He
does?"

"That is a very fair question. You have spoken as if you
believe that Hotoke San really exists as an object of faith and
worship. So I will discuss with you whether that is so or not and
go on from there to answer your question about Christianity."

Japanese tea had been served, and as they sipped the green
tea from the miniature cups the pastor held forth on the Buddhist position from various angles. He spoke of the historical
Buddha who lived and died in India, and then traced the
progress of his teaching through Tibet, China and Korea until
at last it reached Japan. When it did so it was already far
removed from its original simplicity, and through the centuries
in Japan had gathered further accretions which altered it still
more. He went on to tell of the work of Honen, who lived in the
twelfth century and who propagated the doctrine of salvation
through another whom the scholar had named Amida. Said the
scholar, "Amida is the embodiment of the all-compassionate
Buddha, who by virtue of his long training and accumulation
of merit has completed the scheme of salvation." So the mere
repetition of the sacred phrase centred around the name of
Amida was sufficient to assure to the believer all the blessings

of salvation. The pastor pointed out that this was the main emphasis of the Jodo Sect, which had been further developed afterwards by the Buddhist scholar Shinran. But he further told his visitor that Amida was in fact a mystical being, the product of the mind of man; that Buddha had lived and died in India and that there was no record of his having risen again or of his being alive now. Faith in another was essential to man in view of his sinfulness and moral impotence, but if the object of faith was itself nebulous and without actual being man remained in his helpless and hopeless condition.

The time went quickly and Hashimoto San was surprised to see from his watch that he had been talking for two hours on the rights and wrongs of Buddhism. And he was not through yet. His guest had listened patiently, with an occasional nod of the head or an interjected question.

"In Christianity it is different. We start with the recognition of the existence of God. The world as a created entity demands a creator. Even scientists pressing farther and farther back into the beginnings of things come to a point from which they can progress no farther. There they must acknowledge the existence of God, even though they do not call Him by that name. He is the Great First Cause, the great motive force behind the whole of the complex life and existence of the universe. Now this Living and true God has manifested Himself to mankind in the person of His Son Jesus Christ. The birth of Christ is a historical fact. Why, even in Japan Christmas is celebrated on December 25th, even if from a purely commercial angle. He lived a normal life as a man for thirty-three years, with this one outstanding difference: that He was completely without sin. Examine His teaching, examine the record of His life, and you will realise that He lived a perfectly holy life. Why, even His enemies could find no fault in Him, and when they finally arrested Him and brought Him up for trial they had to engage false witnesses to testify against Him.

"His enemies had their way and Jesus Christ was put to death on a cross. Even there He prayed for His enemies, and one of the soldiers watching voiced the feelings of the many when he said, 'Truly, this man was the Son of God.' But there was more in the Cross than merely the unjust execution of a good man. We believe Christ died there instead of us, bearing away our sin, and providing for mankind a perfect salvation from sin. How do we know that? Because the third day after His death Jesus rose again from the dead, and after showing Himself to His disciples returned to heaven where He is alive now. What I am telling you is not a fairy tale. It is based upon well-documented historical facts.

"Because of this we believe that the Christian Gospel is true. Buddhism is the religion of human wisdom. Much of the teaching is, no doubt, good but there is no power to perform. Christianity is based upon the historical facts of the birth, holy life, death and resurrection of Jesus Christ. It cannot be proved that Hotoke San exists, and Amida San is the product of man's mind and without any actual existence. In that Christ died for us on the Cross, salvation is by simple faith and trust in Him without effort of our own."

So the pastor concluded his argument, and the visitor said he was most grateful for the time Hashimoto San had taken.

"I have clearly understood that Christianity is a good thing."

The two men bowed their farewells and the guest left with a warm invitation from the pastor to come again.

The visitor had not progressed far down the street when Komatsu San came running into the room.

"Sensei, d'you know who your visitor was?"

"Well, he seemed to be quite intelligent and well educated and to have a good grasp of the significance of Buddhism."

"Indeed he ought to. He is the priest of the temple of Aiyoji, and a graduate of the Buddhist University in Kyoto."

"Is that so! But he seems young to be the priest."

"Yes, he is the eldest son, and it was understood that one day he would succeed his father as priest according to the normal custom. However, his father died suddenly and he became head of the temple. But there is so little money in the temple these days that he is employed at the village office. So, Pastor, you have held forth this afternoon to a specialist in Buddhism, and told him all about it!"

"Well, at any rate I've told him the Gospel too in plenty."

"Yes, and we'll pray that God will bless it to him."

The visit of the priest marked the beginning of concerted opposition to the Gospel in the village. Not only did he not appear again at the meetings, but it appeared that his enquiry had been with the intention of gaining fuel for an attack upon the Christian meeting. There are five Buddhist temples in

Sawadani village, and each of the four hundred houses in the community had for generations past been linked to one or other of them. In the good old days the priest and his family could live on the patrimony that went with the temple, augmented by the offerings at special festivals and gifts of farm produce. Those easy days had gone and the priests now had to work to supplement their living. What would happen then if the temples "lost" some of these village families to Christianity? The economic position of the priests would be worsened and their authority weakened. So it was a genuine fear of Christianity that drove the priests together to seek means to combat the Gospel and preserve their livings.

As a first step the young priest of Aiyoji gathered together the four other priests in Sawadani, and also invited two from other parts of the same county to what he called "A Conference for the Destruction of Christianity". We have no knowledge of how the discussion went or what arguments were advanced, but certain outward results indicated that the conference was unfavourable to Christianity in general and the propagation of the Gospel in Sawadani in particular. As a first step it was decided to have *naniwabushi* in the large temple in Kasubuchi and to make no charge for admission. This was a vivid and spectacular presentation in song of some of the old historical stories of Japan, and was intended to take the people away from the Christian meetings. For the same reason sermons were preached periodically in the local village temples, and later still as the lines of Christian work became evident attempts were made to copy them. One temple ran a Sunday school and a young people's meeting, but they lacked the ability to keep the meetings going.

Old traditions die hard and the increased activity on the part of the priests commended itself to the village parents. In an occasional gathering in the temple the priest had lambasted Christianity right and left and stressed the responsibility of parents to see that their children did not get caught in the Christian snare. The parents were not wanting trouble and they fell in line right away. Yes, the young people must not go to the meetings; they should be prohibited. So to Sumi San's chagrin it became increasingly difficult for the young people to attend the regular meetings. There thus arose this strange anomaly. When the young people had been wild-living and out several nights in the week to the movies or the occasional theatre nothing at all had been said, no objections had been raised. Yet now that the young people had become serious-minded, exemplary members of the community they were forbidden to attend the Christian meetings which had been the cause of the great change in their lives.

The work of God in the hearts of these young people was a deep thing, however, and they could not lightly deny the Lord that bought them. Such is the inward witness of the Spirit that a man cannot be robbed of it. You may cajole and threaten him, persecute and intimidate him; you may put him in jail, rob him of his Bible and hymn-book, and threaten him with death itself—yet still within his heart there is the inner conviction of the new life in Christ which he cannot deny. Otani San was such an one. Soon after the first meetings the converts had asked for Bibles and hymn-books, and Sumi San had procured these through Pastor Hashimoto's good offices. From the first the mother of young Otani had opposed his faith in Christ. She had forbidden him to go to the meetings, had burned his Bible and hymn-book; but the fire of faith within his heart burned the more brightly. Nor was he alone. Though they were told not to attend the meetings, the young people continued to come after the initial blow had fallen. They would put on their good clothes as if to go to the movies or to visit friends. Sometimes they would go up the hill away from the meeting-place, but make their way round by a circuitous route to the place where faith and fellowship were stimulated. The parable of the Interpreter's House was being re-enacted and the activities of the Conference for the Destruction of Christianity seemed to be badly backfiring.

Now opposition came from another quarter. It was nearly a year after the initial meetings in the village when one day the landlord of the house came to Sumi San. We have mentioned that he was a local Shinto priest, but had so far taken no attitude of opposition to the Gospel.

"Komatsu San, I want to have a talk with you; can you spare me a few minutes?"

"Why, yes! Please sit down!"

"I hate to have to say this and feel very bad about it. I do hope you will not misunderstand me, nor think any the worse of me for what I say." The landlord was approaching some problem or other with typical Japanese reticence and preparing the ground before him. He went on:

"It is about the meetings you are holding here."

"Ah," thought Sumi San, "trouble is coming at us from another quarter. What will he say next?" She did not have long to wait.

"We appreciate these meetings very much and they mean a lot to the young people in our village. Many of them have become wonderfully changed and everybody appreciates that. The villagers are not blind to the fact that the village headman and the schoolmaster both attend the meetings, and thus give their approval to what you teach. The difficulty, however, is this. The Buddhist priests are very angry because the young people are getting too eager about Christianity. The teaching is all right as one aspect of the cultural life of the village, but the priests fear that their livings will be endangered if families as a whole become Christian. As you know, the village has been Buddhist for centuries and we cannot in a moment discard the traditions of our ancestors. For some time past now I have been under great pressure from the priests and some of the villagers. I hate to say this, but they want me to turn you out of the house."

The landlord paused to see what effect his words would have. Sumi San nodded her head and softly uttered a monosyllable in acknowledgment of her understanding his words.

"Now I want to be fair. I appreciate the meetings, for I feel they have done our village a lot of good; and as for yourself, you have proved a very good tenant." He smiled. "But I am under tremendous pressure from the influential people in the village. I am the priest of the shrine, as you know, and they threaten to cut off their contributions to the shrine if I do not ask you to go. What can I do? I have put the matter fairly before you; perhaps you have a suggestion to make."

"First of all," replied Sumi San, "I want to thank you for your frankness and your kindness. I have been very happy here and you have given me every liberty. I am indeed sorry that you should be put to inconvenience on my account, and of course I shall have to find somewhere else. At the moment that will be difficult, but perhaps you will let me stay here and continue the meetings a little longer. I am sure that our God will provide a meeting-place in His own good time."

The conversation continued longer and in more detail, but we need follow it no further. Wonderfully enough, for a time the pressure lifted and the priest said no more about the matter for some months to come.

.　　.　　.　　.　　.

To a church in the midst of temptation Paul had written, "God is faithful and will not allow you to be tempted beyond your strength; but when the temptation comes, He will also provide the way out, so that you may be able to bear it." It was just such a word that our poor, weak nurse needed as she witnessed for Christ in her lonely mountain village. At great personal sacrifice the meetings had been started, and when converts had been given she was responsible for their care and progress. What could she, a poor woman, do? How could she lead them on? True, help came from time to time from outside, and God was wonderfully building up the young converts. Yet still, in one sense, she was alone; and now, a year after the meetings, the blows of opposition were beginning to fall. "Not tempted beyond your strength"—it was a good word, and Sumi San turned it over in her mind as some delightful morsel. It brought strength and comfort to her. God was with her. He would temper the blast; and when it seemed as though strength must fail, there before her would be "the way out". "*Shinjimasu*, I believe," she cried in her heart, and it was faith, and faith alone, that carried her on. She knew what it was to suffer; she had come to the upland of faith through the dark valley of pain and tears. If God had met her then, He would meet her now. The lessons learned in the bitterness of suffering during the days before her conversion were proving their worth now. And Sumi San kept steady in God.

The Conference for the Destruction of Christianity kept up its work and the Buddhist priests now began to work from another angle. Particularly since she had nailed her colours to the mast in organising the evangelistic meetings, Sumi San had gone everywhere preaching the Word. As she carried on her work as health visitor she spoke to her patients about the Lord Jesus and often prayed with them and for them. To the priests it was an intolerable situation and they determined to stop it. Into the village office one day strode the priest of Aiyoji with a fellow priest from a neighbouring temple and requested to see the head of the Health and Sanitation Department. He came out to meet them.

"We are sorry to trouble you when you are so busy, but there is a matter we wish to bring to your notice. It concerns the welfare nurse Komatsu San. It has come to our notice that the nurse is actually using her position in the village as a means of propagating the Christian religion. You will know as a village elder that this village has been Buddhist for centuries, and all of us have been reared in the true faith. Now this nurse has come in from outside, and after waiting her time she starts Christian meetings and has succeeded in deluding a few of the younger and lesser-taught young people. Now, quite openly, she goes from house to house and in the course of her work urges the people to believe on this foreign religion. And all the time she is being paid by village funds which have come from the pockets of good Buddhist believers. We come this afternoon on behalf of the villagers. They want this matter stopped. They will not have their money put to wrong uses, and we ask that you forthwith dismiss this nurse."

The official was obviously taken aback by this tirade and did not quite know what to say.. After a few moments he said:

"I appreciate your coming to see me about this matter. We try to be democratic in this village and conduct the affairs of the community according to the expressed wishes of the people. The nurse has been most satisfactory in her work and has been most sacrificial in her attention to the sick in the village. We do know that voices have been raised in opposition to her of late, but you, gentlemen, will appreciate the fact that her dismissal is a question to be decided by the whole village council, not by this department or by myself as its head. I can do nothing more than refer the matter to our next meeting if that is your wish."

"It most certainly is our wish, and we will exert all our influence to bring about her dismissal."

After further discussion they left, but they were as good as their word. The village was divided over the matter of Komatsu San. Some appreciated her faith and service, even if they did not subscribe to her particular religious belief. Others, as a result of the astute propaganda of the priests, desired nothing more than to see her dismissed from her job and driven from the village. The latter they could not do, for she was free to live and work where she chose as a qualified nurse and midwife. The former they finally accomplished, and it was a sad day indeed for Sumi San when she was called to the village office and told that her services were no longer required.

This was a cruel blow indeed. She well knew that, humanly speaking, everything depended upon her employment in the village as welfare nurse. With the money she had saved from her salary she had started the evangelistic meetings, and with her current income she continued the work. If her employment ceased could she continue to live in the village? If not, then who would care for the little flock still so much in need of shepherding? Her whole programme built in faith in God seemed to be falling to pieces. Could it be that here too "He will also provide the way out"? Sumi San was to prove that even in this most recent blow God was at work leading on and out into larger places. Before that, however, a wonderfully joyful experience was hers as the first converts confessed Christ in baptism.

Chapter 11

"FITLY FRAMED TOGETHER"

As we have traced the outbreak of persecution and the gathering opposition to the Gospel in Sawadani we have hurried along too quickly and must now retrace our steps to record the progress of God's work in the hearts of His children there.

After the initial meetings and Pastor Hashimoto's subsequent visit there were several occasions on which visiting preachers came and brought the Gospel message to the village. Among those who came was Pastor Honda, and it was a special joy to Sumi San to meet once again the one through whom, under God, she had been converted. God blessed the pastor's visit, and outstanding among the converts were three young women—one of whom was the only daughter of Mr. Nitta, the stone-mason. She was employed at the local Farmers' Co-operative and, like others of the young people, found her soul's need met in Christ. But the great decision was not made on the spur of the moment. It was not until the fourth time of hearing the Gospel that her reserve was broken down and she saw in Christ her Saviour. The gracious words "Come unto Me, all ye that labour and are heavy laden, and I will give you rest" won her heart, and she declared for Christ. Thus the number of the saved grew, and as the first anniversary of the commencement of the work drew near many expressed a desire to be baptised. So once again a letter was sent to Pastor Hashimoto, and in response to the call he came to Sawadani in March to examine the converts and prepare them for baptism.

Sumi San met him at the bus stop and together they walked the few steps to the house at the corner where she made her home. After they had entered the house and were quietly sipping the inevitable cup of green tea the pastor remarked:

"Komatsu San, you look tired and your colour is bad. Are you feeling all right?"

"Thank you, Pastor, for your kind enquiry As a matter of fact I am ill. I have had a pain and a swelling in my breast for some time, and a few days ago I went to see the doctor in Kasubuchi. He confirmed what I already feared, that I have cancer of the breast."

"Cancer of the breast, Komatsu San? Surely not that!" cried the astounded pastor.

"Yes, and it is already in an advanced stage."

"Why, then, you must have an operation. Did the doctor not say anything about that?"

"Yes, he said I must be operated on immediately. But, Pastor, I cannot do that, I simply cannot."

"And why not?"

"Pastor, you have come here to prepare the converts for baptism. Suppose I go into hospital now, I shall either miss the joy of seeing these people baptised or else the service will have to be postponed. But there is a more important consideration than that. If I leave here now, these twenty-seven souls who have expressed a desire for baptism will be badly let down. Not only that, but the villagers will misunderstand things, put a wrong construction on the whole matter, and say that the judgment of God has fallen upon me. Pastor, I simply cannot go into hospital until these souls have been baptised."

"Komatsu San, I appreciate your zeal and courage, but is this right? You are greatly needed here in this village and must take care of your health. Would it not be better to have the operation at once? We could postpone the baptismal service until after the summer, and you would be better by then."

"No, Pastor, the Word says, 'Ye are not your own, for ye are bought with a price', and my body belongs to God. He will take care of it. There is another point too, though this is private between us two. Money is scarce, and if I use for the operation the money I have saved I shall have none for the needs of the evangelistic work here. The souls of dying men and women are a more important consideration than the weak body of one poor woman. If I die, I die, but God will sustain me and give me health. As the Psalmist said, 'I shall not die but live and declare the works of the Lord!' "

The pastor was silent in admiration for such faith and devotion, and was so convinced that God was leading His child that he could seek no further to make her change her mind. He marvelled as he saw what God had done in the life before him, and gave praise to God for her selflessness. How completely she had forgotten herself and her interests! She now lived solely for the good of Sawadani village and for the souls of the people there.

It was at this time that the blow fell that we recorded at the close of the last chapter and Sumi San found herself cut off from her source of employment and of income. Her condition could hardly have been worse. She had now no settled source of income, she was economically hard up, and was suffering from a very serious malady. In the spiritual realm she felt herself committed to a continuation of the work of evangelisation in the village; but this required money, and so far the contributions from the Christians were extremely small. A lesser faith would have halted and fallen, but Sumi San's heart was fixed. She knew the will of God and proceeded to do it. Every penny that could be saved was put on one side, and to do this she continually denied herself. Furthermore she gathered up her own clothing and put the garments in pawn. With the money thus raised she was able to invite outside speakers into the village and carry on her mission. She had learned the lesson that "he that loseth his life for My sake shall find it". She was indeed laying up treasure in heaven, though this did not enter into her consideration. Before her eyes were the souls of the lost, and her one passion was to see them brought to new life in Christ.

．　　　．　　　．　　　．　　　．

May Day of 1949 dawned clear and fair in Sawadani village. From the azure blue of the sky the eye followed the sweep of the green, tree-covered hills as they reached down to the edge of the rushing, singing river. To the eyes of many in the village

> *Heaven above was softer blue*
> *And earth around was sweeter green,*
> *For something lived in every hue*
> *Christless eyes had never seen.*

The songs of the saved joined the chorus of nature in praising the One who had made all things new in their lives. Today was baptism day, and the twenty or more who were to make public confession of their faith were full of joy.

It had been agreed to meet at Komatsu San's place for a service at nine o'clock and from there proceed to the Go River. As the hour approached little groups were seen converging on the corner house from different parts of the village, each person carrying a parcel tied up in a square cloth. Hymn-book and Bible were a "must"; a change of clothes and a lunch were also essential, for the place of baptism was two or three miles distant. Ah, there is young Takahashi, his brother and sister—three from one family ready to confess the Lord. And that older man and his wife? They are Mr. and Mrs. Sugimoto, who are later to become stout pillars of the young church. Hearts are filled with joy as the various ones take their place in the little meeting-room.

The opening hymn is a most appropriate one—"Since Jesus came into my heart"—and its joyful sound swells out with real feeling. Prayer and praise mingle during the opening exercises and then Pastor Hashimoto turns the attention of the meeting to Galatians 2: 20: "I am crucified with Christ, nevertheless I live; yet not I, but Christ liveth in me: and the life which I now live in the flesh I live by the faith of the Son of God, who loved me, and gave Himself for me." Baptism was not so much the graduation ceremony as entrance into school; it was not the completion of the life of faith but its beginning. They were not to think that because they were baptised they had attained; they were just starting out and must from then on press on from grace to grace and faith to faith. Indeed baptism was symbolic of death. As they entered the water and were immersed in it, so they had already died indeed unto sin. As they rose from the water cleansed by its stream, so they had already risen to new life in Christ. Baptism was the symbol of the reality, the outward confession of what they already experienced inwardly. Baptism would mark them out still more for attack by the enemy. Immediately after His baptism Jesus had been sorely tempted by the devil, but had conquered in the power of God. They too must be ready for temptation and opposition, but they too could triumph and would triumph in the power of God. With these and other fitting remarks the pastor exhorted the little group, and with further praise and prayer the meeting came to an end.

Then the Christians formed into a line outside and started on the long walk to the river. Nothing like this had been seen before in Sawadani. Anything unusual would attract a crowd anyway, but that morning the folk of Chihara were out in force as the believers marched off singing their hymns. On they marched down the hill, following the road as it wound round the side of the mountain, till at length they came in sight of the Go River. They had been following a tributary stream through its narrow valley, and now the valley widened out to present a beautiful view of mountain and sky and broad, shallow-flowing river. They crossed the stream they had been following and made their way out on to a wide gravel bank that had been thrown up by the main stream in the course of the years. Here was an ideal spot. The clear, sparkling river water flowing fresh from the mountains, the trees on either bank dressed in the new green of spring, and over all the great blue arch of heaven.

The river here was about fifty yards wide and in the centre the stream was quite swift. However, they found a quiet pool where the water was still and prepared to have the baptisms there. Some of the young men had brought bamboo poles to make an enclosure for changing clothes before and after the ceremony. While this was being prepared the older Takahashi boy came up to the pastor.

"Sensei," he said, "will you let me be baptised first?"

"Sa, Takahashi San, I don't know about that. We usually baptise the men first in order of age and then the women after that in the same way. I fear it would be rather out of order for you to go in first. Why do you want to be the first?"

"Sensei, there are two reasons. First, I would not have believed it possible that I could have become so changed in the course of the year. I am indeed a new creature in Christ, and I want to be baptised first as my testimony of thanks for what He has done. Then too I want to be first in faith and first in consecration. I want to go in first to show that I am determined to go through with Christ whatever the cost."

"Thank God for your faith, brother; we'll see what can be done. Hallo! Who are those men coming over the shingle there?"

Takahashi San turned round to look in the direction in which Mr. Hashimoto was pointing. There three men were making their way towards the group of Christians, and from the wisps of tobacco smoke rising into the air it was evident that they were not fellow-believers.

"Looks as though they are newspaper men; they seem to have cameras with them," ventured Takahashi San.

And so they proved to be. They had heard of the work of the Gospel in Sawadani and of the forthcoming baptism and wanted a record for their papers. A Christian baptism of village converts in a mountain stream was an almost unheard-of thing. Later they took photographs and reported the event courteously and with decorum, and the Christians felt that it helped to sound out their faith through the district.

Now hymns of praise were being raised to God as a brief preliminary service of worship was held by the flowing river. The believers to be baptised were committed to God in prayer, and one by one they went down into the river. In accordance with his expressed desire Takahashi San was first and as he came up from the water shouted a loud "Amen" of praise. One after another they followed on, and soon the pastor had to have a break, for he found the river water exceedingly cold. As the baptisms took place a well-known Japanese baptismal hymn was sung by those waiting on the bank, and continued until some twenty-seven souls had thus publicly confessed Christ. Meanwhile quite a few villagers from nearby had gathered to watch the ceremony, and before the service was closed the pastor briefly exhorted them to turn to Christ.

The service over, there was a great deal of hand-shaking and bowing as the baptised believers greeted one another and thanked the pastor. Then they scattered here and there into little groups for lunch and for a time of fellowship in Christ. It was middle afternoon when the Christians reached Chihara again, still singing their hymns of praise and rejoicing in the Lord who had bought them. They gathered once more in the meeting-place on the corner, and there the pastor had some further words of instruction to give them.

"This is a day of great joy to me and of great blessing to you. You have now been baptised and openly declared that you belong to Christ. Komatsu San here has been the means, in God's hands, of bringing the Gospel to this village, and we thank Him for all she has done. It is your turn now to carry on the evangelistic work which she has begun. She has given liberally and sacrificially of her money to finance the preaching of the Gospel. Komatsu San can do this no more. She is ill and will have to go into hospital for treatment, but by your regular offerings you will be able to give enough to keep the work going. The Scriptural method is to give a tenth of your substance to the Lord, and I pray you may all do that."

The believers had not all realised how ill Komatsu San was, and some faces showed surprise and dismay at what the pastor said. He went on:

"The great thing to do is to keep one in spirit and in heart. Don't let the enemy come in to divide you. Choose from among your numbers some who will be leaders among you—a small committee to handle affairs. As soon as possible organise yourselves as a church and hold regular meetings. I suggest that you meet Sunday morning and evening and Wednesday evening for prayer and Bible study.

"You may say how can we do that without a regular pastor? Each of you can share your experiences of what God has done for you and how He is leading you. As you read the Bible, God will teach you and bless you. Pass on to others in the meetings what God teaches you in private. Study the Bible. There are plenty of books to help you in your study, and soon you will be able to preach the Word to others. Above all, keep together, uphold the unity of the Spirit. The devil will oppose you, but you are victors through Christ."

. . . . .

God never lacks His man. It was He who sent Joseph to Egypt to store food for the preservation of the chosen race and later prepared Moses to enter into contest with Pharaoh for the release of their descendants. The defection of Saul found David ready, a man after God's own heart, deeply taught in the solitude of the Judaean hills. When the Persian prime minister sought to exterminate the Jews in the land of their captivity an Esther was ready to intercede. And when Judas Iscariot went out into the night, God already had in preparation the twelfth Apostle of His choosing—Paul the Fearless. Examples of the principle are innumerable, nor are they only adorned by illustrious names that glow bright upon the page of history. After all, it was Mary Jones's desire for a Bible that hurried forward the formation of the Bible Society.

From Sawadani village a young lad had attended school in Iwami-Oda, the large town on the coastal railway. He was staying with relatives during the years of his schooling, and as his hosts had no children of their own he was finally adopted into their family. Prospects for young people in the area were poor thirty-five years ago, and being a youth of initiative and ability he emigrated to Manchuria. Sugimoto San did well there and found a comfortable job in one of the banks in Dairen.

The years passed by, and with the Japanese occupation of the territory and the formation of a government favourable to the conquerors Mr. Sugimoto's position improved still more. He lacked no good thing. Money was sufficient if not plentiful, and he had a happy home with two daughters born into the family. He was far better off than he could have been in Japan, and indeed was living in luxury compared with his friends back home. But then the tidal wave of World War II swept over the Orient and Manchuria was engulfed. Almost overnight the Japanese authorities were ousted and the Russians came to take their place. For a while the Sugimotos were able to continue as usual, but it soon became evident that life was going to become increasingly difficult. He began to study the books issued by the Japanese counterpart of "Christian Science"—*Seicho no Ie* (House of Growth)—in an attempt to to find spiritual peace in the midst of material uncertainty, but with little success.

At length the opportunity to return to Japan was offered to them in common with other Japanese residents. As they attempted to get their belongings together, ready to leave, they found to their dismay that they were forbidden to take their goods with them. Try what they would, the law was inflexible, and they eventually landed in Japan with little more than the clothes they stood up in. Like many another Japanese, it was to his birthplace of Sawadani that Sugimoto San returned, and there, because of the traditional family relationships, he was at last welcomed. He was fortunate too in finding a house in which to live and a job to do at the village office. The few comforts of life that he and his wife were able to gather round them did little, however, to still the yearning cry of the soul within. Of course they were angered at the loss of their possessions, of course they quarrelled with the cruel turn of fate—but that did not bring inner peace.

It was at this time that Sumi San started the meetings in the village, and among those who earnestly attended the meetings from the first were the Sugimotos. Not only so, but in Christ they found the One who could satisfy the inner longing of the heart independent of circumstances. The presence of this educated and experienced man in the little group was a real stabilising influence. Unlike the younger people, he knew the world and its ways, he had tried life without God and found that it still left an aching void within the soul. Now when the church was being organised Mr. Sugimoto emerged as an "elder" of the group. On Pastor Hashimoto's recommendation he bought a Bible Commentary and studied diligently to present to the newly baptised Christians the sincere milk of the Word.

God had His man for such a time as this.

Chapter 12

THE CHISEL OF CHASTENING

THE baptismal service over, Sumi San was now faced with her own personal problem. She must have hospital treatment for the malignant disease that had fastened its hold upon her. Yet how could she go into hospital? She had no funds to draw upon and yet she felt sure that God would not let her down. Prayer was again her refuge and comfort, and her confidence in God remained unshaken.

Deliverance finally came from an unexpected quarter. During her three years of employment at the village office she had contributed to the local insurance scheme in common with the other employees. It was true that her period of service had come to an end, but it was finally established that she was eligible for assistance from the insurance funds. Great was her joy when one day Sugimoto San brought her the news that no less than ten thousand yen would be made available to her.

"That is good news, Sugimoto San. But then I expected the Lord to provide. Do you know that hymn, number 506 in the hymn-book—'The Lord will provide'? I love the last verse of that:

> *God who in the stormy sea*
> *Opened up a way;*
> *God who in the desert dry*
> *Made the manna fall;*
> *He will work His perfect will.*

If God could care for the hosts of the Israelites in such a wonderful way, He can surely meet my need. And now you see He has done it! Hallelujah!"

"You certainly have great faith, Komatsu San. I wish I could have the same. By your kindness and sacrifice the Gospel has come to our village, and now that you are in need we shall stand by you until your health is restored. Now that the money is available we shall have to see about getting you into hospital."

To Sumi San the problem before her was somewhat like that which faced the Apostle Paul. "I am in a strait betwixt two, having a desire to depart, and to be with Christ . . . nevertheless to abide in the flesh is more needful for you." She would gladly have stayed in Sawadani working to upbuild the Christians, seeking to save the lost until the Lord called her Home. Yet she felt that if her life could be prolonged even a while longer it would enable her to finish her course and get the little group soundly settled and rooted in Christ. The decision was at length made and to hospital she went.

Some of the womenfolk from the little group went with her, and the journey took them first by bus to Kasubuchi and thence by railway to Hamada. The journey took about four hours and Komatsu San was quite weary by the time they reached their destination. In many Japanese hospitals it is still the responsibility of the relatives or friends of the patient to care for the cooking and give general attention, the nurses meanwhile looking after the medical side of things. Komatsu San had no relatives near her, but there were those from Sawadani bound to her by spiritual ties, and of these two agreed to remain initially to care for her material needs.

Meanwhile back in the village the Church Committee called a meeting of all members. Sugimoto San took the lead. He explained that they all felt a sense of responsibility towards Komatsu San, for they were in her debt spiritually. She had at great sacrifice to herself scraped and saved her money and pawned her clothes so that the Gospel could come to their village. She was now in the hospital in Hamada and desperately needed help. He told of the ten thousand yen which had come from the insurance, but explained that this was insufficient to meet her total expenses. So there was need of financial contributions in the first place. Then someone was needed to care for her while she was in hospital. He presumed it would be difficult for anyone to be there all the weeks that treatment was being given, but perhaps they could take it in turn. Even if they could not give money in large amounts, gifts of food and vegetables would be most welcome.

The response was immediate. The young people had become deeply attached to the quiet little nurse, and she was to them a true mother in Israel. Now it was their privilege to minister to her in material things, and minister they did. For the two months or more she was in hospital she never lacked an attendant, some staying a couple of days, others a week or ten days. Visitors she had in abundance, and they never came empty-handed. Little packages of rice and eggs, together with gifts of vegetables, all found their way to Sumi San's room in Hamada Hospital.

It was on 24th May 1949 that the operation was performed for the removal of the cancer. The doctor's report was a very grave one indeed. Treatment had been badly delayed and it was too late to accomplish a complete cure. He gave Komatsu San just seven months to live, at the end of which time the disease would again overtake her. The news saddened her spiritual children in Sawadani, but nothing could dampen the faith and fervour of Komatsu San herself. Whether she lived or died she was the Lord's, and her work was the Lord's.

Much prayer had gone up for Sumi San during the operation and the post-operative period, and her faith and joy were the amazement of all in the hospital. One day, some days after the operation, the doctor came in on his routine visit to examine her. He found her with a quiet spirit of praise in her heart and said:

"Komatsu San, how do you keep so bright and cheerful in the midst of so much suffering? You must be in a good deal of pain, and yet I do not hear you complain. You seem to be different from my other patients."

"Doctor, I used to be like other people at one time and did plenty of grumbling and grousing in my day. But I came to an end of myself and put my trust in Christ. Now day by day I have a deep peace in my heart. I have committed my life into His hands and He guides me in the way that is best for me. Peace is a natural gift when the responsibility of one's life is in the hands of God who is love."

"Your faith is certainly a wonderful thing and I wish I could have it too. I have studied Christianity a little bit but did not seem to understand it."

"Ah, doctor, faith is higher than reason. Even a child may believe. It is the simple child-like heart that is needed."

"Perhaps you're right," said the doctor as he passed on.

Hamada Hospital is a large hospital with several hundred

beds, and serves a wide area; but Sumi San's faith was noised abroad throughout the whole building. The nurses who attended her began to tell others, and from different parts of the building patients who could walk about came to see her. Paul could say that "the things which happen unto me have fallen out rather unto the furtherance of the Gospel"; and even though he was bound, Christ was manifested throughout Caesar's household. So it was with Komatsu San; confined to bed though she was, the witness she gave to Christ spread far and wide. Of those who came to see her she asked the same question, "Do you know why I am like this?" and proceeding from there preached Christ.

Among her visitors was a young fellow who had been with the Japanese forces in China. Over there he had had a tough life and returned thoroughly disappointed. When he went into battle he, in common with his fellow-soldiers, had worn "the band of a thousand knots". This was a long broad piece of cloth for wrapping round the stomach, knotted in red cotton with a thousand knots. He was told it would ensure safety in battle and immunity from death. Yet he saw his fellows fall and die on the battle-field. He had been told that Japan was invincible, that the gods would give victory, and yet he had seen the Japanese armies defeated and he and his fellows had been returned to a homeland occupied by alien forces. His homecoming too had been a disappointment. No hero's welcome for him. In disgrace and ashamed, he had returned to find little food and no work. No wonder that he had fallen victim to the subtle propaganda of Communism. He found in it an outlet for his energies and became so aggressive that he came under suspicion by the police. It was then that he had a bad attack of liver trouble and had to enter hospital. When Sumi San was witnessing there for Christ he came to see one who, independent of material circumstances, was filled with peace and joy. She was able to communicate to him the secret of her happiness, and though he had many questions to ask these finally ceased and the dissatisfied soul found lasting peace and satisfaction in Christ. In addition to that, he found in one of the girls from Sawadani his future wife, and now married they are giving a good witness for the Lord.

Into Sumi San's room one day came the pastor of the local Holiness Church, Mr. Hoshino. He had been visiting one of his own believers in hospital and word had come to his ears of the witness of the little nurse.

"You will not know me, but my name is Hoshino and I am pastor of the Holiness Church here in Hamada. It is good to hear of your faith in Christ. Have you been a Christian long?"

"For several years now, *Sensei*. I am glad to meet you too. I came to Christ under the ministry of Pastor Honda in Kobe."

"Oh, Pastor Honda! Why, I have heard of him, although I have never met him. Do you know Mr. Sawamura and Mr. Ojima?"

"Why, yes. I have several times heard their messages in conventions in the Kobe area."

The two found they had many things in common, not the least being their mutual love for Christ.

From then on Pastor Hoshino took Sumi San under his wing as if she were his own church member, and Sumi San for her part was glad to know of the existence of a Gospel witness in the city of Hamada. She told him of the work in Sawadani and of what God had done there, and he in his turn told of the hardness of the work in Hamada and how few attended the services.

"Joseph is a fruitful bough, even a fruitful bough by a well; whose branches run over the wall" sang Jacob in his latter years. Now in Hamada the fruitful bough of Sumi San's witness ran over the wall and began to influence many outside the hospital. She was only too happy to introduce enquirers inside the hospital to Pastor Hoshino's church. Her stay in the town was temporary, while those among the nurses and patients who had found Christ needed a spiritual home. Behold then this wonder! A poor weak nurse suffering from malignant cancer and confined to her sick-bed gives such a witness for Christ that in the course of the ten weeks of her stay some thirty people are saved, both nurses and patients! These, introduced to the local church, carry the fire of a new enthusiasm with them, and the languishing group there is revived and quickened into newness of life. Where previously only four or five people were attending the meetings, now the meetings are alive with new vitality. Not only so, but in later years two of those who were saved at this time offered themselves for full-time service and went into the work of the Lord.

"God hath chosen the weak things of the world to confound
the things which are mighty."

.   .   .   .   .

Meanwhile things were happening in Sawadani itself. To go
back a little, the immediate result of the baptismal service was
increased persecution of the young Christians. Photographs of
the baptismal service and an account of Komatsu San's work
had appeared in the local newspapers. This meant that the
village had overnight become in measure important, and
newspaper reporters came once and again to ask Sumi San
about her faith and her work. They felt they had a human-
interest story of news value and they made the most of it.

To the young Christians this was a great encouragement.
Hitherto they had been despised and misunderstood, but now
they featured in the Press and the news of their faith and of the
work of their beloved leader was published far and wide. This
gave them great boldness of faith, and they openly testified
again and again to Christ and His great salvation. To the
villagers it seemed that nothing could stop the enthusiastic
spread of the new faith, the whole world seemed to have gone
after Him. However, the zeal of the new converts was only
equalled by the determination of the villagers to quench the
fire of faith, and they did all they could to hinder things. The
Christians for their part called on the Lord to behold their
threatenings and with all boldness preached the Word.

With regard to Sumi San's removal to hospital the village
folk had mixed feelings. They were sorry to lose the kindly
midwife from their midst and were genuinely grieved to know
of her serious condition. Yet there were those who felt that her
going would probably help resolve the problem of the Christian
movement in their midst. Remove the leader and the followers
would scatter. His enemies had so reasoned with regard to the
Great Leader and His followers. But this thing was of God, and
the little group had the power of divine life within it. The
villagers therefore were surprised to observe that the Christian
meeting continued, indeed thrived in the absence of its leader.

Some of the thinking members wondered how the midwife
would manage in hospital without relatives to care for her.
Then to their amazement they saw their own young people
making the four-hour journey to Hamada, staying in the

hospital and in turn caring for Sumi San, and all at their own expense. Moreover, they did it with joy and delight and seemed almost to compete with one another for the privilege of helping the invalid. Previously these same young people had been selfish and wilful, spending their spare time in seeking their own pleasure and interests. Whence then this great change? No Japanese would fail to appreciate the public spirit behind the intention to help someone in real need, and in this particular case they could not deny the fact that the motive power was Christianity. Whether it were right or wrong, desirable or undesirable, a foreign religion or not—this Christianity had certainly wrought a good work in the village young people. And with this appreciation persecution for a time came to an end.

. . . . .

Pastor Hashimoto and the other interested pastors in the Kobe area were keenly exercised about the continuation of the work in Sawadani, and by prayer and effort did all they could to help forward the work. Particularly was this so when Sumi San had to go into hospital and they envisaged the little group without experienced help of any kind. About that time an itinerant pastor whom we shall call Mori Sensei came into the picture and seemed to be God's answer to the problem.

Mori Sensei had been active in evangelistic work for some years before the war and was now without a church and therefore free to help out in Christian work anywhere. So he was asked to go to Sawadani and help in the services there. His needs were few, his position only temporary, so that he would be no great burden financially upon the little group, and they received him gladly, happy to have the assistance of one taught in the Word of God.

To know Mori Sensei was to know his message. He was a melancholy man, deeply introspective and frequently moody. His face was drawn and sad, his voice low and heavy, and his closely cropped hair seemed almost indicative of the state of bondage in which he perpetually lived. His name was Legalist, and legal were his views and legal his doctrine. No doubt he would not have denied that salvation is by the grace of God, but he had built up in his own mind a series of prohibitions that continually reiterated "Thou shalt not!" This was a very different presentation of the Gospel from that which the believers had heard from Sumi San and Pastors Hashimoto and Honda. There was joy in their message, released from the bondage of sin and fear and doubt. Their Gospel produced a song, Mori Sensei's produced a sigh; and before long the believers were entangled in the toils of legal bondage—"touch not, taste not, handle not!"

"Beware of covetousness" was one of his watchwords; and when asked to be more particular in his interpretation, he stated, for example, that to overeat was covetousness. It is the very nature of the truly born-again soul that he accepts the Word of God at face value, and the teaching of accredited pastors as truth to be believed and followed. Never does the Bible speak so definitely, so clearly, so very much to the point, as it does during those early days of one's first love. And the desire to perform is there and the will to do it. So it was with the Sawadani believers. Did the Word teach that to overeat is covetousness? Then they would not eat at all, or only in small quantities, lest the work of God in their hearts be hindered. Before long parents were amazed at the sudden diminution in the amount of good their sons and daughters consumed in their apparent lack of appetite. When, upon enquiring the reason, they were told that Christianity prohibited healthy and hearty eating, the parents' anger and opposition flared up again, and once more the believers faced misunderstanding and opprobrium.

Thank God, there is an antidote for legalism. Paul faced a similar problem in the Galatian churches, and his epistle to them is the Spirit's answer for all time to those "entangled again with the yoke of bondage". Legalist continued his ministry for four months and then left. Following his departure Pastor Hashimoto came again to Sawadani and, taking the Galatian epistle as his text, preached unto them Christ. "Stand fast therefore in the liberty wherewith Christ hath made (you) free." Their chains fell off, joy returned, and the spirits of the believers soared up and on with their Great Deliverer.

The time had now come for Sumi San to leave hospital, and with her discharge and temporary return to Sawadani we enter upon a new stage in God's mighty work there.

PART III

LIVING STONES

"Ye also, as living stones, are built up a spiritual house . . . acceptable to God by Jesus Christ."
(1 Peter 2: 5)

Chapter 13

A BROADER FOUNDATION

UPON her discharge from hospital it was obvious to Sumi San that no cure had been effected. The immediate growth had been removed, but the fibrous tissues remained that could spread out and cause trouble again at any time in another area. The doctor had given her seven months to live, and she asked only one thing—that she might spend that time labouring for the Lord in Sawadani. She had no fear of death and no concern for her own physical well-being except as she could use her given strength for God's glory. The house at the corner was still available for use, and as a midwife she could continue to earn small amounts sufficient to live and carry on her evangelistic enterprise. But God had other plans.

The Psalmist in calling upon all nature to praise the Lord uses a phrase of particular significance—"stormy wind fulfilling His Word". He pictured the raging stormy wind lashing the earth, uprooting trees, toppling the frail houses of man, and sinking the ships of his construction; and back of it all he realised that even the stormy wind was fulfilling the Word and accomplishing the Will of God. The same is true of our lives. Unless we reckon upon the master mind of a God of Love behind the happenings of world, life becomes a meaningless, inscrutable problem which does no more than raise countless questions in the mind of man. But view the storms of life, the seeming wrack and ruin, frustration and loss as all fulfilling His Word, and life takes on a rich and full significance.

Sumi San found it so. In the next months events transpired that almost seemed to thwart her cherished plans for the last months of her life. Yet the stormy winds were fulfilling God's Word, and by the time she peacefully entered the desired haven God had done far, far greater things than she had ever anticipated. That is the story that must now be told.

What a welcome Sumi San received when she returned to

Chihara that summer of 1949. The Christians had set her rooms in order and decorated them tastefully with chrysanthemums. The villagers too were not unmoved and were there to welcome her on her return. She looked somewhat pale and thinner, but her friendly smile was still there and her dedicated will moved her steadily forward in God's plan and purpose. Of course there had to be a thanksgiving service when praise was given to God for His gracious restoration of His child, and Sumi San too expressed her gratitude for the loving care bestowed on her by the Christians of the village.

"What are you going to do now, Komatsu San?" asked one of the Christians.

"Why, just keep right on working and witnessing here in Sawadani, as long as the Lord gives me health and strength," she replied. But God purposed otherwise.

Newspaper reporters continued to come and visit Komatsu San and the work in Sawadani, and occasionally wrote up the progress of the Gospel in their papers. This had one rather startling result. The reports were read by one of the masters in Matsue University, the city nearest to the scene of Sumi San's labours. He was a Buddhist priest, but like many another was having to work for his living. Stirred by the reports of the entrance of Christianity into Sawadani, he wrote an open letter to the paper in some such words as these:

Dear Mr. Editor,

I have read with interest and with shame the reports in your esteemed paper of the entrance of Christianity into Sawadani village in Ouchi-gun. Though Christianity has had considerable success in the more populated areas of our country, this is the first time that it has gained a footing in the predominantly Buddhist mountain areas of our prefecture. Already we priests whose ancestors built and manned the local temples are in difficulties owing to the high cost of living and the decrease in income caused by the exodus of so many young people to the big towns. If this religion of foreign origin continues to spread in this area our patrimony will well-nigh cease to exist. In large measure this is our fault and demonstrates the weakness of the priests in Sawadani village. It seems to me that something is seriously wrong when the five priests in the area cannot turn Christianity out. Their strength cannot be very great if they give in to one single nurse. It is time we did something about things.

Respectfully yours,

. . . .

This letter was naturally enough read by the five priests themselves and they were greatly incensed by it and by the shame cast upon them. They therefore redoubled their efforts to get rid of Sumi San, and by roundabout means again brought pressure to bear upon her landlord to turn her out. He, poor man, was between Scylla and Charybdis—anxious to help a sick woman in her plight, but driven almost to distraction by the insistence of the influential villagers, backed by the priests, that the Gospel-propagating midwife should go. At length his decision was made and Sumi San was told that she must leave the house. This, of course, raised several problems: where would she live, where could she work to earn a living, and where could the Christians meet? The obvious thing was to air the matter in a general meeting of the believers, and this was duly called.

Sumi San opened the proceedings, and after hymn and prayer said:

"Friends, you will recall that last year, before the baptismal service, great pressure was brought upon me to leave this building. At the time I appreciated the fact that the landlord was in a difficult position, being the priest at the local shrine, and yet at the same time permitting us to have Christian meetings in his home. I therefore agreed to move out when a suitable place became available. However, at that time I was taken ill and had to go to hospital, and the problem was temporarily shelved. Now once again I have been asked to move out owing to the opposition of the Buddhist priests in the village. Not only that, but I am told that our hymn-singing is a nuisance to the neighbours, though I find it hard to believe that. So I'm afraid I shall have to leave. That raises at once the problem of where we shall continue our meetings, and I have called this gathering so that we may discuss the matter together. The final answer to this problem is of course for us to build our own church building. That is a big piece of work, but I have saved up eight thousand yen which I will gladly donate to start the work. I'm afraid it is not quite enough, but it will help. Now I would like to know what you feel about the matter."

There was silence in the room for quite a while, each one, with native Japanese reticence, waiting for the other to speak first.

Then Sugimoto San spoke up and said:

"We are not surprised at what you have said, Komatsu San. It was evident that sooner or later we should have to find a permanent building for our meetings, and we must now give serious thought to this problem. We are most grateful for your kind offer of financial assistance. You have done so much for us, indeed everything for us, up to the present. And now once again you take the lead and set us an example. I don't know where we are going to get the money to put up a building, but I'm sure that as we all give as we can and pray earnestly God will provide the means. It almost seems as if He is leading us to take this step, I feel."

Takahashi San followed on:

"I'm sure we all appreciate Komatsu San's great offer, and we must all seek to match her giving with our own sacrificial offerings as unto the Lord. As the Psalmist said, 'What shall I render unto the Lord for all His benefits toward me?' I feel there is much we young people can do to help build a church. We shall need lumber and stones, and we can cut the one from the hills and gather the other from the river bed. We can work hard and give our time, and together can put up a house in which we may freely worship God."

This was greeted with general agreement and considerable enthusiasm, and it became evident that to erect a building was not so much beyond the reach of possibility as they had at first imagined. Finally it was decided to form a small building committee which would look into practical matters and give advice. It was also agreed to consult with Pastor Hashimoto as to the most suitable type of building and other related matters. Once again it became evident that God had gone before, and in choosing their committee the Christians found they had just the men they needed. There was Sugimoto San, employed at the village office and well versed in the legal side of things. His acquaintance with figures rendered him of great value also in estimating and assessing both money and materials. Nitta San, the mason, was available with expert and experienced knowledge of how to lay foundations and to do cement and stone work. Old Mr. Hasegawa, a Christian of many years, had returned from Korea to live in Sawadani and had been revived and quickened by the meetings there. He was a carpenter by trade, as was also one other, and carpenters would certainly be needed. One of the Takahashi brothers ran a sawmill, and all the young men knew more or less about hauling wood from the hills. God, who for a more stately edifice had prepared Bezaleel and Aholiab, had also His prepared and appointed workers in Sawadani. So the Building Committee was formed.

They met several times, and as they did so their faith grew. At the first meeting Sumi San raised her offer to fifteen thousand yen, and almost felt in her eagerness that this would nearly "foot the bill"! They gently told her that this amount was not nearly sufficient. At first they thought of building a house of rough-hewn logs, but then it was felt this would be too small. As they prayed over and discussed the matter their faith rose until they felt at length that they should go ahead and build a proper church with accommodation for a pastor.

There was a reason for their wishing to build an apartment for a pastor, for God was already preparing one to lead the flock. The older Takahashi boy had felt the call of God to full-time service and was preparing to enter the Bible School in Kobe. Pastor Hashimoto had visited the little church in the early part of 1950 and had talked long and earnestly with the young fellow. He it was who had wanted to be first baptised—"first in faith, and first in consecration" as he had said. From the out-set he had gone on steadily with God, giving a grand testimony in his home and in the district. Said the pastor:

"You know what this means, Takahashi San. This is not a little thing, something temporary. To consecrate yourself to God's service is a lifelong job. First of all you will have four years' study in the Bible School and from then on you will have to look to the Lord for the supply of your daily needs. A pastor has no guaranteed income. His life is indeed a life of faith. The time will come too when you will want to marry, and then children will be given you. Can you trust God for them as well as for yourself?"

"Pastor, I have thought a great deal about this and prayed about it too. I feel that God has called me, and that He will see me through. My burden is to come back here when I have graduated and minister to this group where I first saw the light of salvation. I know I can do nothing; but the Word says, 'He whom God hath sent speaketh the words of God', and I am looking to God to fit and equip me.''

"Well, if you are sure that God has called you, I know He will see you through. Pray much about it and make your decision before God. The school year begins in April and you could write for application papers any time. Now let us pray over this very important matter.''

The pastor laid his hand on the shoulder of young Takahashi and feelingly committed him to the Lord. He had passed that way himself and knew something of the disappointments, trials and temptations which would confront him. He also knew that nothing mattered so much as a clear call from God, and he prayed earnestly that the young fellow might have that without a doubt.

In meeting with the little group in Sawadani the pastor was able to advise them and confirm them in their decision to build a church, and they determined to go forward in faith and prayer. Until, however, a church building could be completed where were they to meet? Sugimoto San came to the rescue and opened his home for the gatherings, and there during building operations the believers met and their faith was maintained and stimulated. Across the road from Sugimoto's house a clear stream of sparkling water flows out of the hillside, and in the home time and time again the believers drank of the life-giving water of the Spirit.

Before he left to return home the pastor was quietly talking to Sumi San one evening and asked a natural enough question.

"Komatsu San, where are you going to live and what are you going to do from now on?''

The nurse smiled at him in a quizzical fashion and replied:

"I've been thinking and praying about that. I have no house here now, and I feel that is an indication that God is sending me to Kobe.''

"To Kobe!'' cried the pastor in astonishment. "You can't go to Kobe in your condition; and if you went there what could you do?''

"I'm not so weak, Pastor, as you think. I have already been in touch with my friends down there, and there is a post vacant for me in a nursing association in Ashiya. There I hope to live and work, and the money I earn I can send back here to help build the church. The little group can get along without me now. Sugimoto San is doing very well in Bible Study and the other young fellows are growing in grace. With your help from time to time things will run along nicely, and I will pray all the time for Sawadani and my brethren in Christ there."

The pastor did not know what to say. Here was a sick woman, with seven months to live, prepared to go out into the city and work to help build a church for the worship of God in that mountain village! He did his best to dissuade her, but she would not be moved. She was convinced of God's will for her personally and had set her heart to do it. At length the pastor agreed.

"Komatsu San, I cannot dissuade you from this course of action and can only bow my head before the will of God. The God who sends you has said 'Certainly I will be with thee!' and in His will you will be safe and secure. Do please take care of yourself and don't take unreasonable risks. I am in Takasago, the other side of Kobe from Ashiya, and if I can help you in any way let me know."

"Thank you, Pastor. I know the Lord will see me through."

There were two farewells in Sawadani Church that year. Takahashi San's application papers had been favourably reviewed by the Bible School authorities and towards the beginning of April he made the twelve-hour journey to Kobe. There was quite a crowd at the bus to see him off, and the mountain valley resounded to the singing of "We'll fight till Jesus comes" as the vehicle left for the journey to Akana. There they changed buses, for some of the young men were going with him part way, and journeyed on to the railhead in Hiroshima Prefecture, passing near Sumi San's home village on the way. At Miyoji he entrained, said final farewells, and set off on the rail trip which lasted the rest of the day.

As the sun set in the west he made his way up the steep winding hill to where the Bible School building stood looking over Japan's Inland Sea. Soon he was inside, sitting at the evening meal with some thirty or so young men from all parts of Japan. Like Takahashi San, they all had heard the call of God and were there for training for His service. Later he was shown his room, which he shared with another brother; and as he went to sleep that night his surroundings were as quiet as his native village, except for the "pom-pom, pom-pom" of the engines of the fishing-boats busy at work out at sea. So Takahashi San entered upon his four-year course of training—training that he might become a true "fisher of men".

The other farewell was for Sumi San much later in the year. They would not let her go without promise of an early return, and not without repeated exhortations that she take care of her health. Once again there was the crowd at the bus, the songs of praise at the farewell, and off she went to Ashiya. As she passed the village office she could not help but think of the time, five years before, when she had waited for a bus at the stop right there. Then it was that a "chance" conversation had led her to Sawadani, and with what blessed results. She was leaving behind her a keen group of believers, one of whom had already entered Bible School in training for pastoral and evangelistic work. Her health was gone, her future unpredictable, but if it was at all possible she wanted to return to Sawadani and die there. Later in the day the train carried her along the foot of the hill on which the Bible School was built, and she lifted her heart in prayer for her son in the faith living and studying there.

Thus she arrived in Kobe, and there it was that she learned that her husband of former days had returned to Mikage on his sudden disappearance after they had left the city. His madness had apparently increased more and more, until eventually he died a raving lunatic. Sumi San herself found a quiet and happy sphere of work in association with the other nurses in Ashiya, and after a few days was sent to care for a rich elderly lady living in a well-appointed house in that town.

Chapter 14

BUILT IN PERILOUS TIMES

THE major problem connected with the erection of Sawadani church was finance. No matter how keen their desire and their willingness to help out with practical work, how could the Christians build without money? So the committee met to assess their financial position.

"How much exactly have we in hand?" asked Sugimoto San.

"Well, we have the fifteen thousand yen donated by Komatsu San, but that is about all," replied the treasurer of the committee.

"That will not last long. Now the point is: how are we to raise the money we need? Our members are not very well off; and though we always have vegetables and rice produced in our own farms and have enough to eat, ready cash is hard to come by. Has anybody any suggestions?"

"I wouldn't mind going out to the mountains and trying to catch weasels. The village office will pay from a thousand to two thousand yen for the pelt. How about making traps and seeing what we can do?" suggested Ueki San, one of the young men.

"That's an idea, and it should work provided the Lord guides the weasels into our traps," said another with a laugh.

"Could we run a stall at the time of the village festival and sell rice-cakes, toys and so on?" ventured another.

"I think you have a very good suggestion there, and one in which the womenfolk can help," said Sugimoto San. "Let's see, when is the festival?"

"About a month from now, so there should be good time to prepare, and with the villagers coming from all parts we should do a good trade."

Then another fellow spoke up. "I've been thinking that I could work up in the hills a bit during the slack season, and I'll be glad to donate what money I made to the building fund. It may not be much, but it will help a little."

"Thank you, brother, that will be fine. Let us do all we can, give all we can, and most of all pray all we can. Then we shall find that our building problem will become a spiritual blessing to us. Now I suggest we meet again in about a month as a committee and see how finance is coming in," concluded Sugimoto San.

"May I make another suggestion before we finish?" interjected Nitta San, who seldom spoke in the meeting. "Where are we going to build the church? This valley is so narrow and there is so little level ground that we are going to have great difficulty in finding a site. All the arable land is taken up for fields and rice-paddies. I think we should start right now and look round for a suitable and central site."

"Thank you, Nitta San. I think we should accept that suggestion and see if we can turn up something by the next time we meet. Any other business tonight?"

There were no other suggestions, so the committee adjourned but the good work initiated went on. A few weasels were caught and the proceeds of their sale went into the building fund. Some of the young people went out to the cities to work and sent back what they could to help in the building. The sale at the time of the village festival exceeded all expectations and the proceeds helped swell the fund. And once again from Ashiya there came a liberal contribution from Sumi San, who day and night laboured and prayed with one thing in view— the erection of the Sawadani church.

Soon the treasurer reported that the sum of forty thousand yen was in hand, and it was felt that a start could be made in gathering together the necessary material. Stout beams would be needed for the uprights and crosspieces, so some sixty were bought, but the purchase completely knocked the bottom out of the treasury and no money was left. But from then on the money came in little by little, and the Christians never plunged into a debt so great that they could not see the way out.

The question of a site was, however, a very real problem. One evening when the committee met someone suggested that the ground at the base of the village fire-tower might be available. A couple of hundred yards up the road from the corner house where the meetings had been started the red steel structure stood which housed the fire-bell. In the event of fire the bell was rung with a rhythm which varied according to the proximity of the fire. The pylon stood on a piece of stony ground some twenty feet above the roadway. One of the Takahashi boys and Ueki San went down to see the site, and there under the tower they prayed that God would give them the land if that was His appointed place for the church. The site was central enough, but how elderly folk would be able to climb up to the place presented a real difficulty. However, in the end God provided some better way.

It was Watanabe San who made the suggestion that eventually led the Christians to the place of God's provision.

"My father has a small field alongside the road half-way between Chihara bus-stop and the fire-tower. I wonder whether he would rent us the land or let us buy it cheaply."

"That sounds good. Whereabouts exactly is it?"

"D'you know the little path that runs in by the side of the old Co-operative building to my place?"

"Yes, quite well."

"Well, it is just there on the left. I think you will find that it is just large enough for the building we have in mind. It is a rice-field just now, but being on high ground would drain quickly. It has this advantage too, that it is just off the main road and there is already a path leading to it."

"Will you ask your father about it and see what he has to say?"

Watanabe San agreed to do this, but the whole problem of getting the land bristled with technical difficulties.

Watanabe San found that his aged father was only too glad to offer the land, and would lease it to the church until such time as they could buy it. But—and it was indeed a big BUT—the land had been allotted to Watanabe San under the redistribution scheme after the war. By a decree of General McArthur land was taken from large land-owners and given to the farmers, so that for the first time many of them owned the land that they tilled. Previously they had frequently had to pay extortionate rents, with the result that the farming class was in perpetual debt and poverty. To prevent the return of land to the moneyed people, and the wholesale cornering of property, legal restrictions had been enacted which made sale and resale most difficult. Not only that, but if the land were used for building purposes it would go out of food production, a thing frowned upon in food-hungry Japan.

The law required, among other things, that for sixty days before the sale public announcement should be made of the intention of the owner to sell. This enabled other interested parties to speak up and express their desires. When the intention of Watanabe San was made public there were indeed other interested parties, and they were not favourable to the Christians. A rich land-owner whose field lay adjacent to the proposed site of the church wanted the land for his own use. The priest at the Hachiman shrine was not interested in buying the land but was extremely keen that the Christians should not get it and thus establish their work in the village. And these two joined forces to keep the land out of the hands of the Christians.

For days the necessary papers circulated from village office to town office to county office, and meanwhile prayer was made without ceasing unto God by the Christians. And God answered prayer in a wonderful way. At the crucial time the rich land-owner was ill—indeed he was laid up for some six months and could take no further interest in the land. Then for some reason or other the land-owner and the priest came to blows, and so anxious did the latter become that the land-owner should not get the land that he threw his weight into the church's application, with the result that it was granted! God had once again made the wrath of men to praise Him!

And now the Christians set about the work of church-building in real earnest. Whereas they had thought of buying a shack as a meeting-place for about twenty thousand yen, they finally realised that it would cost them three hundred thousand yen to build what they had in mind. Even then they would need to do all the labouring themselves. The believers were all young people, none of them with homes of their own, and the few grown-ups were repatriates who had a struggle to live. Seven of the believers had left home to work in Osaka so that they could earn more money. They hated to part with their fellow Christians in the valley, and tears were shed as they left; but each one worked hard sending home money to his own people, and sending extra as an offering to help build the church. Indeed they worked so faithfully and hard that the heads of their firms began to ask what the influence was behind it all. When they learned the secret they decided that they would have all their employees from Sawadani!

At the same time those back home matched the sacrifice of those who had gone to the cities with their service for the Lord, and strong in faith looked forward to the day when the church would be built. They did so too in the face of severe persecution. In some cases they were beaten and scolded, and some were turned out of their homes. They were not even allowed to attend one service during the week, and so they waited until their parents were asleep; then, with their footwear in their hands, they stole out of the house and ran to the church for a little time of fellowship. Some were even denied food upon the supposition that they were being fed at the church(!) and some lost weight because of this. The opposition in some cases went so far that parents would not give them needed warmer clothing, with the result that the young folks suffered. Yet their faith burned ever more brightly and God was glorified.

With such opposition it was impossible for the young people to give any time during the day for work on the church-building, and of necessity they had to labour at night. So we see them leaving their homes dressed as if to go to visit a friend or on some pleasure jaunt. As soon as they arrived at the appointed place they changed into their working clothes and started off for the hills to cut wood.

"Ah, Ueki San, you have done well to come tonight. How did you manage to get out?"

"I tell you, *kimi*, I had a hard job. That older brother of mine seems determined to keep me away from the church; but as I came home from work I saw the red paper was out on Sugimoto's place, so I knew I must do my best to come and help in the work tonight."

"But you're all dressed up as if you were going to a show or something."

"It may look like that, but thank God I've been saved from that. I've put off the old man. Watch . . . "—and so saying he slipped off his good clothes and was ready for action and hard work.

It should be explained that the Christians had devised a series of signs by which they communicated with one another as to whether a labour force were needed on any given evening. Along Sugimoto San's garden there ran an old tile-topped fence. On this Sugimoto San posted sometimes a red circle of paper—workers needed tonight; or a white circle of paper—

workers needed tomorrow night; and so on. Thus, without the necessity of informing one another by word of mouth and thereby incurring suspicion and opposition from their parents unnecessarily, they organised the continuance of the work.

"Everybody ready now. Where's the hand-cart?"

"Over here," replied someone out of the night.

"Anybody carrying the food?"

"Yes, it's tied on the hand-cart."

"O.K. Make sure it does not fall off. We'll need that before we get back again." There was a general laugh all round.

"Saws, axes, wedges, ropes all loaded O.K.? Sugimoto San, you have the lantern, and the extra matches too? We shall need them for a fire."

"Yes, everything is in order here."

"Fine! Then let's go. What is the time? Just 9 p.m. Well, we have about eight hours to work before daylight. Quietly through the village, remember, and then you can sing as much as you like when we get to the mountain."

Silently they moved through the village, where the lights were going out one by one as the farmers went to rest. The moon shone fitfully as the large fleecy clouds scudded across the sky. Soon they were away from the houses and pulling hard up the narrow mountain road.

"Halt! This is the place. Unload the gear and pull the barrow into the side here." The younger Takahashi made a good organiser, and the believers followed his leadership well.

Through the night they laboured felling and trimming the trees, cutting them into required lengths, and singing as they worked. Sometime in the early hours of the morning they stopped and had a meal. A fire had been kindled to make tea, which helped wash down the rice-balls the size of a man's fist which the boys had brought for their meal. Then on with the work again. Great care had to be taken in the dark in felling the trees, but God wonderfully preserved them all from harm. Then suddenly the first song of the birds would be heard, and the grey light of dawn filtered down through the trees of the forest. And as the men looked at one another they laughed, for overnight they had turned into old men, their hair and eyebrows being covered with white hoar-frost!

"Oi, *kimi*, what's happened to you? Your hair is as white as snow," chaffed one.

"People who live in glass houses shouldn't throw stones! You're just as white-haired yourself. What time is it?"

"Nearly five o'clock. How quickly the night has passed. Oi, Takahashi, we ought to be getting back."

"You're right. Come along, let's load the cart and get going."

Down the narrow mountain road the boys went, hanging on to the cart for dear life lest it should get out of control as it swung round the corners. It was still early when they passed through Chihara, and then came somewhat of a pull up to where the Takahashis' elder brother had a sawmill. This was journey's end for that night. The wood was left there to be trimmed and planed and later carried to the church site. It was indeed God's provision, this mill of the Takahashis. The Christians were able to get their wood prepared at cost price, and the younger Takahashi boy was well acquainted with the method of preparing the lumber in the forest.

The Christians now began to look round for stones suitable for using in the foundation of the building. River stones might be good enough as ballast for cement, but shaped stones were needed for setting into the foundation. Away up the side road from the corner house in Chihara was an old tumble-down building. At one time it had been a dwelling-house but it had long since fallen into disuse. Here was an ample supply of ready-cut stone just ideal for the church foundation. Some of the men of the church approached the owner and they were given the freedom to take away what they needed. The only problem was the distance to the church site.

So at the dead of night a procession of slowly walking figures might have been seen making its way down the road to the river, across the river by a temporary bridge and up the other side to the building site. When the night was dark, lamps were placed at intervals on the ground to guide the carriers, or some who could not do the carrying held lanterns to guide those who were shouldering the heavy stones to the place of building. When the river was in spate it was necessary to take the longer road round by the corner meeting-place. And thus the stones for God's house were provided.

One of the joys of the Christians during this year of preparation was when Komatsu San appeared again in the village on a short holiday. How glad they all were to see her, and how rejoiced she was to see the way preparations for the building

had gone forward in her absence. She was moved to tears as
she saw the Christians going off at night to the hills to cut
lumber: and though they did their best to dissuade her, nothing would do but that she also accompany them. Careful
record was kept each day of those who joined in the work and
how many hours they laboured, and Sumi San's name stands
on that roll of honour with the rest.

So the year of 1951 passed, and at length a sufficiency of
lumber was ready to make a start on the building. But before
that could take place the site had to be prepared. A rice-field
that has been flooded from year to year does not make a suitable building site without considerable preparation. The soft
top-soil has to be removed and the ground hardened before
the solid foundation is laid. So little by little the surface earth
was removed and the stones that had been brought from the
old building laid in place. This again was all done by night by
the light of a bonfire of wood chips and shavings, or, failing
that, by the flare of gasoline lamps.

In the spring of the following year Pastor Ojima was invited
from Kobe for four days of special services centring around the
laying of a foundation stone on the site. The pastor brought
the Christians just what they needed—some solid instruction
in the Word of God, of which he is an able and experienced
exponent. Then one afternoon they all trooped out to the
church site and a simple service of dedication was held. Hearts
were full of praise to God as they gathered for the little ceremony which really marked the actual start of the long-awaited
building of the church.

Chapter 15

BUILT BY NIGHT

Now the time had come for the actual laying of the foundation, and this was a really big problem. In building a house in Japan community help is needed on two occasions: one in the preparing of the foundation and the other in the actual erection of the framework. At these times the villagers come together and work with a will, and are rewarded with rice-cakes aplenty and rice-wine in liberal quantities. The Christians needed this community help right now, but they were a misunderstood minority who at the moment did not command the goodwill of the villagers. Nor had they money with which to hire labour. How could they man the thirty or so ropes which raised the heavy wooden hammer to pound the stones into the trench for the foundation! They could probably not muster half the number. However, they must do the best they could, and hope that the God whom they served would give them help to complete the task. To add to the problem the ground was extremely hard, as there had been no rain for a month or more, rendering it difficult to pound the stones in.

A day was fixed in the late summer. All hands were to be on deck in the evening as soon as the regular day's work was done. The day came and rain poured down without cessation, making it impossible for them to get on with the job. So they agreed to meet the following day. By 6 p.m., the appointed time, there was no one on the site; by 8 p.m. still no one present. At last even the long summer day was waning and it was about 9 p.m. By that time fifteen had gathered and they prepared to make a start. They built a fire in the centre of the lot to give light and gathered round it to sing and pray before they started work. Then all went to the ropes with a will and, singing and shouting, started their massive task.

They had hardly started, however, when from the direction of the village the sound of voices and shuffling feet was heard, and soon at the church site appeared a crowd of young men with towels tightly tied round their heads. Still they came, more and more, until something like seventy to eighty were present. Somehow the Christians by their steadfast resolve and steady work had won the approval of the village people, and the young men had turned out in force to help them in the preparation of the foundation. Soon all were working with a will, and in the space of two hours the work was finished and the workers were not even tired. Of course there was no strong drink for the workers, but they managed along on liberal quantities of green tea; and although the congratulatory rice-cakes had not been prepared, the men renewed their strength with some huge rice-balls.

The work over, they all sat round the huge bonfire.

"*Yare, yare!* We have finished in double-quick time, thanks to the young men of the village."

"Yes, and thanks to yesterday's rain! Why, it made it so much easier to pound in the stones. Fancy, no rain for thirty-five days, and then just before we prepare the foundations God sends us that wonderful rain. He truly is with us in this project."

"The old proverb says that 'rain hardens the ground', but yesterday's rain was certainly a rain of blessing as far as we are concerned."

Suddenly someone began to sing "I will cling to the old rugged Cross", and soon all the believers joined in. Tears flowed freely as they considered God's present mercy and His great love at Calvary, and it seemed natural that Takahashi Torao San, back home from Bible School on vacation, should lead in prayer before they all dispersed. Thinking of it afterwards, he said:

"In the dark night the fire rose high as did our songs of praise. As we who had worked together had literally made the earth to move, so it seemed as though the sound of work and praise reverberated through the village. Eventually about a quarter of the people in the village had come to see what was happening, for in the still night the sound of the singing sounded far and wide. Afterwards the old men of the village said they could never recall such a foundation-laying, and once again God was glorified in the believers."

.   .   .   .   .

In the village of Sawadani there are, beside the five Buddhist temples, no less than three Shinto shrines. One of these is within a short distance of the church site and is dedicated to Hachiman, the god of war. It must have been the outstanding advances the Christians were making that stirred up the priest to take action too. In the early weeks of their church-building efforts the Christians had been the laughing-stock of the villagers. Nehemiah had similarly been mocked when he and his people had commenced to rebuild the walls of Jerusalem —"even that which they build, if a fox go up, he shall even break down their stone wall." But Nehemiah had persisted and the wall was finally completed. So too in Sawadani; the villagers' mocking and laughter took on a really hollow sound as before their very eyes the lumber and stones were prepared and the foundation laid. They could not deny that the Christians had something—real character and backbone that enabled them to press through their difficulties.

So the priest of Hachiman decided that they would rebuild the shrine which had fallen badly into decay. Apart from the spring and autumn festivals, the occasional wedding and so forth, the building was not much used. But what could better put the Shinto shrine into the foreground again than to rebuild it and improve its outward appearance! So the campaign was launched with a dinner-party given by the priest to the influential men in the village, and there it was decided to solicit subscriptions from all the homes in the community. This would soak up any surplus cash that might otherwise find its way into the Christians' hands and also promote a renewal of interest in the Hachiman shrine.

The campaign went with a swing. There seemed to be no scarcity of cash in the village when it came to rebuilding the shrine. The priest gave liberal promises of prosperity in business, protection from illness, and blessing on home and hearth to those who contributed, irrespective of whether he could implement them or not. Eventually they gathered something like five hundred thousand yen into the rebuilding fund. However, it became necessary for the influential members of the committee to meet frequently to discuss plans. Each meeting meant plenty of food to eat and plenty of rice-wine to drink. The more they drank the less they seemed to gree on the procedure to be followed in the reconstruction. So of course another meeting had to be called and yet another, while each gathering and the feasting that accompanied it gradually used up the money collected.

At length the matter came to the ears of the villagers.

"Well, wife, they're off again tonight!"

"Who are off?"

"Why, this famous committee of men who are seeing to the rebuilding of Hachiman San. I don't know how many parties they have had already, but I have just seen them pile into a bus and leave for Yamanaka Hotspring. That's where our money is going: into feasting and o sake, into parties and geisha. It'll be a wonder if any at all is left to carry out the reconstruction."

"Well, can't we do anything about it?"

"Who's going to do anything or say anything? All the leading men of the village are on the committee, and they get so fuddled with drink that the more they discuss the less they agree. It's the disgrace of the village! Now look at those young Christians. It may be a foreign religion and a new one to our village, but I tell you they have backbone and character. Ridiculed and opposed though they are, they go out on the mountain night after night cutting wood or else carting stones, and out of their small wages give what they can to their church. I know, I've laughed at 'em too, I've ridiculed and opposed them, thinking Christianity was bad for our village; but I'd sooner have them than those sake-drinking committee members. Mark my words, they'll have their church finished while Hachiman San is still thinking about the repairs to the shrine."

"I believe you're right, father. What impresses me is the happy way they go about it too. You'd think the way they've been treated that they would have grumbled and groused; but not so. They always seem happy, and you can hear them singing their hymns as they work away. I must say I rather like those hymns too. I wouldn't mind going down to some of their meetings when their church is finished."

"Couldn't do any harm, anyway. I'm through giving money to this Hachiman project. If I have any spare cash I'll give it to the Christian church. They at least deserve it!"

Such sentiments were common throughout the village in many a home, and when it became known that the committee members had squandered some two hundred thousand yen on their parties the villagers were "hopping mad". Pressure was brought to bear on those responsible and the remaining money was put to the purpose for which it was donated. The most they could do, however, was to put a new roof on the shrine—a very much lesser accomplishment than had been foreshadowed in their grandiose plans. Meanwhile the Christians were praised throughout the community, and as it became evident that their preparations were solid and dependable a contractor was willing to take over the construction of the church. Small amounts of money also were handed in by the villagers and new people began to attend the regular meetings. Once again Satan, the Adversary, had overstepped the mark, and God was glorified in His children.

.   .   .   .   .

The summer of 1952 passed into the golden autumn, and after the rice-harvest had been gathered from the fields—early in that part of Japan because of the long winter—the ridgepole-raising ceremony took place on the church site. It is the custom in Japan for all the beams, uprights, crosspieces and so on for use in the building to be prepared on vacant ground adjacent to the site. They are slotted and fitted in such a way that in a single day the framework of the entire building can be set up. This again is a community project, and this time helpers gladly came forward to help the Christians raise their building right up to the ridgepole. The heathen place some sprigs of evergreen and paper prayers on the top, to ward off evil spirits and cleanse the place. The Christians instead had hymn-singing and prayer, and with praise and thanksgiving committed the embryo building into God's hand.

There was still much to be done. The more the contractor saw of the work of the Christian young people the more he was impressed. It encouraged him to put his best work into the building too. At times he would mention to young Takahashi that he needed certain lumber by the next day if the work were not to be held up. That day the red paper would be posted outside Sugimoto San's house, and by nightfall the men would be ready to go out to the mountain and cut the wood required. All through the night they worked, and by next day the wood was ready at the building site. Not once did they have to lay the carpenter off through lack of funds or material. Every one helped and worked with a will, even the women holding lamps on dark nights while the men worked.

No wonder the villagers were impressed.

"Oi, what time is it?"

"Just past three o'clock, father," replied a sleepy voice from the other side of the quilts.

"I thought I heard a barrow go by. Who'd be pushing a barrow at this time of night?"

"It'll be the Christian young people, I expect, hauling lumber from the mountains for their church."

"A-ah, how I admire them! I tell you, wife, they have backbone and character. Well, another couple of hours' sleep. A-ah!"

Some of the villagers seemed almost ashamed to think that these young people were outdoing them in zeal and hard work. Others of the young people who were enquirers heretofore came into clear faith and assurance of salvation as they mingled with the saved young folk, so that spiritual blessing went hand in hand with the material building of the church.

Gradually the church took shape, and it was the Christians' hope and wish that they might be able to have services in the building by Christmas. There was still a great deal to do, especially in the line of cementing and plastering. The days were cold now, yet night by night both young men and women worked carting up stones from the nearby river. Frequently the girls felt their feet would freeze as they paddled around in the mountain stream gathering the stones together. The boys, on the other hand, were sweating as they carried the heavy loads of ballast up to the building site. Even the married women helped, for time and again there were bowls of hot noodles to refresh the willing workers part way through the night.

Other nights were spent in the hills obtaining the soil which, mixed with chopped-up straw, would be used for plastering the walls. Soil, water and straw are mixed together and trodden by foot until the right consistency is obtained. Owing to the opposition of their parents the young people could not use their rubber boots, and by the light of gasoline lamps trod the mud barefoot. It was bitterly cold, and at times their feet were swollen and even bleeding. Yet they did it all with joy. Perhaps they were thinking of Him who for their redemption had trodden alone the winepress of the fierceness of the wrath of God.

And so December came and with it Christmas. God rewarded their faith and labour, and the building was sufficiently completed to permit of services being held in it. With the coming of the New Year of 1953 the Christians welcomed Rev. Goro Sawamura, the principal of the Bible School in Kobe, for four days of special meetings. God was in the midst and wonderfully blessed the Christians, and also called new souls unto Himself. Many in the village were impressed and led to enquire the way of salvation.

April had been fixed as the time for the dedication of the church, but somehow or other a kind of lethargy now took hold of the Christians. The building was erected and was in use, though not complete, and it seemed as though they were satisfied with things as they were. Takahashi San had returned regularly when on vacation from Bible School and thus kept in close touch with the progress of the work. Now he sensed from letters that zeal seemed to be flagging and that the work was not progressing as it ought. Perhaps it was a kind of reaction after the tremendous output of labour and the strain of the continued opposition. Takahashi felt he should return when the school year ended in March and sent a letter to that effect. However, a reply came back urging him not to return to Sawadani. There had been torrential rains such as could not be recalled in living memory. Bridges were washed out, the roadway had crumbled away, and it was doubtful if he could get through. But he reasoned that if a letter could make the journey so could he. And so he did.

He took the main San-in line which brought him to the railway station of Hamahara. From there there was no conveyance at all. The devastation occasioned by the rain and flooding was apparent everywhere—trees uprooted and washed down the hillsides, boulders in the paddy-fields, stone walls broken down—and it was evident that thousands of yen would be needed for repair work. Takahashi San set off to walk the rest of the way to the village and arrived to the surprise of everybody. His three years at school had done wonders for him. Not only did he know the Lord in a deeper way but he knew how to preach the Word and expound its truths. He called a meeting in the church a few evenings later.

After the usual time of praise and prayer Takahashi San spoke.

"I want to speak this evening for a little while from the Old Testament book of Haggai, chapter 1, verses 7 and 8—'Thus saith the Lord of Hosts; Consider your ways. Go up to the mountain, and bring wood, and build the house; and I will take pleasure in it, and I will be glorified, saith the Lord.' Then again in chapter 2, verse 4—'Yet now be strong ... and work : for I am with you, saith the Lord of hosts.'

"The circumstances of this prophecy are as follows. The children of Israel, who had returned from captivity under Ezra, had started to rebuild the temple of God with great zeal and enthusiasm. But after a while a great deal of opposition arose and the work of building came to a standstill. The temple might have stood as it was, half completed, for a long time if it had not been for the impassioned preaching of the prophet Haggai. He found the people dwelling in comfort in their own homes while God's house lay uncompleted. He argued that the reason the people were suffering from drought and poor harvests was because they had forgotten the work of the house of God and settled down in leisure. So he urged them to 'Consider their ways' and to get busy building the house of the Lord. God so used his servant that, as we read in chapter 1 verse 14, the leaders of the people were stirred up and the work was soon completed.

"Now in this passage I see a parallel to our own position here. By God's help you have all done wonderful work, so that tonight we meet in our own church building here in Sawadani. But the building is incomplete and we need to stir ourselves again to seek the Lord and His help to complete what we have begun."

Takahashi San went on to speak in detail and exhorted them to consider their ways before the Lord, and then press forward in the work. Half-way through his talk the last bus passed up the road on its way to Akana, and shortly afterwards Nitta San came into the church and sat down on the floor with the others. Takahashi San had learned previously that some thirty thousand yen was still needed to enable the church to be completed sufficiently for the dedication service to be held; but where was the money to come from? The recent flood damage had made it impossible for the farmers to help. Then someone had suggested that perhaps they could borrow the money from Nitta San's employer, who was a public-works contractor. He probably alone in the general area would profit by the storm and flood, for his firm would be called upon to repair the damage done.

So Nitta San had been commissioned to see his employer and sound him out on the proposition of a loan. Now the meeting was over and Takahashi San turned to him and said:

"Well, Nitta San, have you some good news for us?"

Nitta San held up a thick envelope and said simply, "Here it is!"

There was an immediate chorus of "Amen" and "Praise the Lord!"

"Then he agreed to loan it to us, did he?"

"No, better than that. He has given it to the church!"

"What! Thirty thousand yen—a gift. Really?"

"Yes. Really, and without doubt!" and Nitta San, the man of few words, told the story of how his employer had refused to make the church a loan but had made an outright gift of the thirty thousand yen. Did the employer see in the storm damage which brought him profit the good hand of the gods? We do not know; but the Christians certainly saw God's hand in this liberal gift, and once again we see the "stormy wind fulfilling His Word", and very literally so.

The work in the church now went forward with new vigour, and in due time the building was completed. However, a convenient season for a service of dedication had passed for the time being, and it was decided that September 1st should be the date of the official opening.

Meanwhile the Christians looked through their records of labour donated during the building of the church. They found that in the aggregate both men and women had made no less than 676 appearances for night work, while in the daytime the aggregate count was only 220. It can truly be said of Sawadani that it is a church built by night, but built to be as a city set on a hill that cannot be hid.

Chapter 16

OVERLAID WITH GOLD

THE home to which Sumi San had been sent in Ashiya was a typical Japanese residence of the better middle-class, situated on a slight eminence overlooking the sea. The house was set in its own grounds, which were enclosed by a high fence capped with heavy tiles. Entrance was made through a roofed gateway which, though ponderous in size and weight, matched perfectly the general lay-out of the buildings. Once inside there opened to one's sight a typical Japanese garden, with pine trees, bamboos, and azalea bushes tastefully arranged and ornamented by stone lanterns and specially selected rocks. The whole gave almost an extensive appearance to a comparatively small area, and a sense of peace and calm in striking contrast to the bustling world without.

The old lady of the house had been taken ill shortly before Komatsu San's arrival at the Nurses' Home in Ashiya and was proving most trying. She was as old and shrivelled as a dried plum, to use the Japanese simile, and in spirit was cranky and crotchety in the extreme. Nothing would please her or suit her, and with all her money nothing seemed to bring her joy or peace. The younger members of the household were distracted; they did not know how to handle the old lady. Their only hope was that she would soon pass away and relieve them of their burden, but the old lady clung tenaciously to life, well enough to give continual trouble and yet sick enough to demand constant attention.

Into this house came Sumi San, not well indeed herself, but with a will to work and a desire to be helpful. After a few days it became clear that the old lady was responding to Sumi San as to no one else. Somehow she had a way with her, and by her cheerfulness and unfailing patience was able to humour the old lady. The latter was not desperately ill, so that the actual physical care of her was light—just fitted indeed to Sumi San's limited strength. On the other hand the daughter-in-law and other members of the house were delighted to find someone who could satisfy the imperious whims of the old lady, and Sumi San was retained as permanent nurse. Her remuneration was good and Sumi San was able to send money monthly to help build the Sawadani church, and in the good purpose of God she continued in the same home for the greater part of two years.

Sumi San did not miss the opportunity of presenting the Lord Jesus to the old lady and had many a tactful but serious talk with her.

"Honourable grandmother, you have lived many years."

"Yes. If I live to next year I shall observe my eightieth birthday."

"God has been good to you in giving you health and strength for so long and in giving you the blessing of so many children."

"I don't know whether it is the goodness of the gods. I have always worshipped Hotoke San faithfully, so I expect his help and protection," answered the old lady curtly.

"And now, honourable grandmother, does Hotoke San give you peace as you come to the end of the way? Does he give you a hope for the next world?" pressed Sumi San.

"Nurse, I've done the best I can. The only thing I hope for now is that when I am dead my children will not fail to offer incense and prayers and pray for the repose of my soul."

"And if they should fail to do that, honourable grandmother, have you no other hope?"

"Nothing except the mercy of Hotoke San," replied the subdued old woman.

"Listen, honourable grandmother, I believe in Christ as my Saviour and God. Have you ever heard of Him?"

"I know there is a religion called Christianity. It is the religion of the West, of the Americans. It does not concern us Japanese. Buddha and Confucius are the sages of the Orient, and from the days of our ancestors we have followed their teaching." The old lady was emphatic and decided in her views.

"Grandmother, I am a Japanese too, but I have found great peace and joy in Christ. For many years my life was filled with sorrow and frustration and I cursed both God and man. Then I learned that Christ could give peace of heart and deliverance from hatred. I learned that when His enemies executed Him

He prayed, 'Father, forgive them, for they know not what they do', and I asked God to give me that same love in my heart. And He did and my life has become completely different.''

The old lady listened carefully, and at last said:

"Nurse, I have noticed that you are different. You seem to be cheerful all the time, and you have more patience than other people. Do you say your God has done this for you?"

"Yes, He has indeed made me a completely new woman. And, honourable grandmother, a few months ago I had a very serious operation; indeed I might have died as a result. Yet I had no fear of death, but a deep, deep peace in my heart. Jesus Christ rose again from the grave the third day and then ascended to heaven, and because of this He has conquered death and those who believe in Him have no fear of the grave. If I were to die tonight I know I should go to heaven where Christ is. That is a real, shining hope to me."

"I think I would like to have such a hope too. You must tell me more about this some time, nurse."

Sumi San was not slow in taking advantage of the suggestion, and she set herself by prayer and witness to win her patient. God honoured her faith, and at last the old lady found the Saviour and, with her hope in Him who became dead and is alive for ever more, passed out into eternity. How Sumi San rejoiced in the salvation of this soul! It had been worth coming from Sawadani to live and work in Ashiya that this hardened, obstinate soul might be brought to Christ. Not only so, but throughout her two years in that lovely home God had sustained her physically and she had been able to contribute materially to the work in Sawadani.

Now it became evident that Sumi San must move. Her work had come to an end in Ashiya, and she began to look around for further work, meanwhile committing her way entirely to God. It was in October 1952, just before the erection of the church in Sawadani, that she accepted a position as health visitor in Oyama village, not very far from the town of Ikuno. From Ashiya, where she had been living, Sumi San journeyed by train through Kobe westward along the coast to the town of Himeji. Himeji lies about ninety minutes by train from Kobe and is dominated by an ancient castle which is kept in a wonderful state of preservation. There she changed to a train which ran north away from the coast, climbing steadily up and up the narrowing valley until at length she reached her destination. Oyama village lay at the foot of the mountains, and Sumi San was soon at home again among her beloved mountain folk.

Her house was one of several built by the village to house schoolteachers, and it was not long before Sumi San was witnessing to her neighbours of Christ's power to save and satisfy. The wife of one schoolteacher in particular was absolutely filled with jealousy, imagining that her husband was having an affair with one of the lady teachers. The whole thing was quite a scandal throughout the village, but Sumi San did what she could to tell of Christ and of His power to change the heart. After some weeks of praying and witnessing she felt the time had come for a positive presentation of the Gospel in the community. Once again an invitation went out to her esteemed pastor, Hashimoto Sensei, and he came up and held special evangelistic meetings. As a result the jealous wife, among others, was saved, and her humble confession and changed life speedily settled the scandal.

The blessing in the village greatly rejoiced Sumi San's heart, and she had great hopes for the future of the work there. Unlike Sawadani, the village was a prosperous one with large houses, and fields which produced bountiful crops. It would be easy to build a church here, she thought. The money would surely be forthcoming without the work and labour that had been necessary in Sawadani. Moreover, Sumi San was rapidly winning the confidence of the people by her cheery personality and faithful service, and many a one had a good word to say for the new health visitor.

In this way six months happily passed by, but towards the end of that period Sumi San felt increasingly unwell. She was troubled by pain in her shoulder and the swelling of her hand and arm. At length she had to have medical attention, and the doctor told her that the cancer was breaking out again, this time in her neck. However, Sumi San would not give up, but carried on with her work and witness as long as she could. Her method of life was sacrificial in the extreme. As a midwife she frequently received gifts of *o mochi* (pounded rice-cakes), specially prepared to celebrate the birth of a child. Rather than spend money on rice she would eat these, with an occasional cucumber or egg-plant to add flavour. She saved every penny she could, even paying Bible School expenses for Takahashi San. It would have been perfectly reasonable for Sumi San to have used her hard-earned money to ease her own suffering by means of special drugs and treatment. But no! All the time she thought only of others and of seeking first the Kingdom of God.

This state of affairs could not, however, continue and her body became weaker and weaker. At length, upon the advice and persuasion of Pastor Hashimoto, she gave up her job in April 1953 and went into a Catholic hospital near Himeji. Her condition was critical and it seemed evident that she could not live long. Special medicine from America was procured and used in the treatment of the disease, but her blood-pressure gradually became lower and lower. She had for so long starved herself to give her money to the work of God that she had no reserve strength at all.

On the other side of Himeji lay the town of Takasago where Pastor Hashimoto's church was situated. From there once and again the Christians came and donated their blood so that Komatsu San might have blood transfusions. The Christians of the church took her on their hearts in love and prayer and visited her frequently. Nor was she forgotten by the people of Oyama village. Her six months' residence there had endeared the little nurse to them, and until the time of her death they sent gifts of money to help with her hospital expenses. And when the teachers at the Bible School heard of her need and sent monetary gifts her gratitude exceeded until she was almost ashamed. "It is unthinkable that those famous teachers should send money for an unworthy creature such as I am."

Nor was Sumi San's witness silent in spite of her weakened condition and suffering. The patients in her ward observed her quiet and patient faith and listened gladly to the hymns sung by visiting Christians. When the pastor came and prayed with her, conversation ceased and those nearby listened reverently. Thus it was that here again Sumi San's witness bore fruit, for she was able to lead to the Lord the young woman in the bed next to her. Sumi San's fruitful bough ran out over any and every wall, and fruitage was natural, for she was constantly abiding in Christ.

Chapter 17

GLORY FILLS THE HOUSE

WHILE Sumi San lay ill in Himeji Hospital news reached her time and again of the progress of the work in Sawadani, and her joy was full as she heard of the completion of the building. Takahashi San also made it his business to visit Sumi San when his studies permitted, and he always had first-hand news of the church. How they loved to talk together of the past few years and of what God had done! Sumi San was continually asking about this one and that one, and of their progress in the faith. Like a true priest of God she constantly bore upon her heart before the Lord those who through her instrumentality had been brought into the Kingdom of God. Through Takahashi San too she heard of the tentative arrangements to have the dedication of the church on the first of September.

One day she broached the subject to him.

"Takahashi San, I understand the church is to be dedicated on the first of September."

"Yes, Komatsu San, that is the arrangement at present. You will be praying for us then?"

"Torao San, I want to be present at the opening of the church, and I have faith that God will strengthen me enough to make that possible."

"Do you really have that faith? The Christians are most keen that you should be present, but having heard of your serious illness they felt that it was quite out of the question. Shall I tell them that you plan to come?"

"Yes, you may tell them that and ask them to stand in faith for me for a real touch from the Lord so that I can make the journey."

"I'll do that." Then, after a pause, he said, "Komatsu San?"

"Yes!"

"I've been thinking. I shall be leaving school for the summer vacation about the beginning of July. Do you think you could travel home with me then?"

Sumi San thought a while before replying. She was evidently praying quietly to the Lord in her heart. At length she said:

"I believe that is of the Lord. That shall be our prayer target. We will pray that God will strengthen me sufficiently to journey to Sawadani and the church opening. My joy will then be full, and I will go back to heaven and meet the Lord there."

Plans were made accordingly, and with the careful hospital treatment her condition generally improved a great deal. There was no recession of the cancer and a further operation could avail nothing; but her physical frame had been strengthened to match her firm will. With the coming of July the doctor was approached and, knowing the incurable nature of the disease, gave permission for her removal to Sawadani.

One afternoon early in July Takahashi San appeared at the hospital just outside Himeji city as previously arranged, and found Sumi San sitting on a bench in the waiting-room. Her smile was as cheery as ever, though a trifle pathetic, for the growth on her neck kept her in constant pain. She was dressed in a simple summer kimono as it was very hot, and a bundle tied in a square of coloured cloth was beside her.

"Excuse me for keeping you waiting," greeted Takahashi San.

"Not at all. I have not been waiting long."

"Are you ready to go now? If so, I will get the hospital office to call a taxi and take us to the station."

"I'm quite ready to go any time now," replied Sumi San.

Several of the nurses and patients who knew the indomitable little nurse were at the porch of the hospital to see her off. Her stay in the institution had been a bare four months; but God had blessed her witness there and they were sorry to see her leave.

The taxi soon brought them to Nibuno station, where they took train for the first part of their journey. As the train climbed the steady ascent to Ikuno it passed through Oyama village, and there again a few of those who had been helped by Sumi San were waiting to wish her well and speed her on her way. She was seeing them for the last time on this side of glory, but faith in their common Lord Jesus assured them of a reunion in heaven. Over the pass travelled the train and down into the valley again where they joined the main San-in line. There was quite a wait here and it was possible to get some refreshment before proceeding on their journey.

Then all through the night they travelled on and on west to Shimane Prefecture and Sawadani. Takahashi San knew how weak Sumi San was and could only guess how she would stand the journey. Fortunately they were able to get seats, and as the passengers thinned out along the way Sumi San was able to curl up on two seats and get some sleep. Takahashi San sat up and dozed fitfully. Sometimes, when he wakened and looked across at the pale face and still form of the nurse, he wondered whether she were still alive, or had slipped off to glory in her sleep. "Lord, help us through! See us safely to our journey's end!" was his constant prayer through the night. And all was well, for God knew that the race of His servant was not yet fully run.

With the coming of daylight they arrived at Matsue, and another couple of hours or so brought them to Iwami-Oda, where they transferred to the Akana bus. Sumi San was terribly tired, but she had wonderfully stood the journey for one so ill and weak. A temporary resting-place was found for her in the room at the back of the church, and there the Christians welcomed her and lavished every kindness upon her. None could tell how much longer their beloved nurse would be with them, and they grieved as they saw her weak and suffering condition and poured the more love on her. She was back home, among those who were truly her people—"For whosoever shall do the will of my Father which is in heaven, the same is my brother, and sister, and mother."

Within a few days the Christians took Sumi San to what was to be her last earthly home. Above the bus-stop in Chihara was a little tile-roofed, one-storied house—indeed it is still there. It was an unpretentious place with its one six-mat and one four-and-a-half-mat room, but it was habitable and centrally situated. It was obvious, however, that Sumi San needed constant care, and once again the Christians were ready. They engaged an elderly woman, Mrs. Nakajima, and she lived with the little nurse and attended to her needs. These latter were few. The cancer was in the throat making swallowing difficult, so that Sumi San could eat but little solid food.

So the summer passed and the time drew near for the

dedication of the church. Takahashi San was able to be there, though he left a few days later to return to his studies at Bible School. Pastor Hashimoto had been invited to conduct the service, and to assist him Pastor Nagashima from Okayama made the journey over the hills and valleys to Sawadani. Mr. Nagashima had heard of Sumi San and of her work and witness. He knew too that her days were indeed numbered, and that the disease was inexorably strengthening its hold upon her body. As he travelled in the bus he began to think of this one life sacrificed to carry the Gospel to a mountain village. Truly a corn of wheat falling into the ground, dying, and bringing forth much fruit. Gradually the words began to form themselves into a poem, and by journey's end the pastor had crystallised the life-work and mission of Sumi San into the following poem.

> Just a single grain of wheat
>   Falling in the ground,
> By its death a harvest meet
>   Causeth to abound.
> So our Saviour on the Cross
>   Gave His Life away;
> Bearing by that seeming loss
>   Fruit until that Day.
>
> So may we with Christ our Lord
>   Fall a living seed
> To the ground, unseen, unheard,
>   Crucified indeed.
> Thence again may there arise
>   Fruit an hundredfold,
> God's great power to wondering eyes
>   Clearly to unfold.
>
> Let us then go forth again
>   To the barren field,
> Counting neither loss nor pain
>   Seek a heavenly yield.
> Strengthened by the Living God,
>   Casting self aside,
> We shall win from hardened sod
>   Fruit that shall abide.

The day of the dedication dawned bright and clear, and once again the great blue arch of the sky reached from side to side of Marsh valley. The rice-fields were just beginning to take on a yellow hue as the brilliant sun hurried the grain on to maturity. It was the 210th day, but no storm or wind ravaged the quiet mountain village and the farmers were thankful.

From morning the Christians had been busy cleaning the church building and tidying up the ground around it. Fresh new straw matting was spread on the floor of the church, imparting to the atmosphere a subtle smell as of new hay. Above the platform hung a plaque written by Mr. Sawamura with the Japanese characters for "God is love", while on both sides of the reading desk lovely bunches of flowers made a colourful display. A secondhand organ had been purchased, and this completed the minimum necessary furnishings.

The church was full for the service, and with all the guests sitting on the floor it was possible to pack in a large number. Not only were the villagers themselves there in force, but the chairman of the Village Council and the chairman of the Education Committee were present too. This latter was the priest-cum-schoolteacher who had for so long rented the corner house to Sumi San, and by his presence he demonstrated that his sympathies were without doubt with the Christian movement.

Hearts full of praise burst forth into singing as the opening hymn was announced. It mattered not that the organ-playing was imperfect, for God has ordained praise even out of the mouths of babes and sucklings. And there was every cause to render thanks to God for what He had done in the hearts of so many and in the building of the church. Later in the service Sugimoto San was called upon to give some statistical details of the finance handled and the man-hours of labour given in the building of the church. As it stood the church was free of debt, but there was still need to tile the roof and make other improvements. Indeed Komatsu San had a tremendous vision for the village. More than once she had spoken of following the building of the church with a parsonage, a kindergarten, an old people's home, and finally a hospital. It was obvious she could never carry this into effect, but perhaps others would be burdened to complete what she had begun.

Komatsu San herself was on the platform in a place of

honour but almost slumped into the chair, so weak was she. So Hashimoto Sensei helped her to her feet, and there she stood supported by the pastor and holding on to the reading desk to steady herself. Then the pastor said:

"It is a great joy to us all to have Komatsu San with us today, and indeed the service would not have been complete without her. We have been hearing from Sugimoto San of all that the Christians have done by their gifts and labour to make this building possible. But let us remember that there would have been no church here at all had it not been for Komatsu San —indeed there would have been no Christians here either. A little more than five years ago I was asked to come here for the first Christian meetings to be held in Sawadani. God blessed at that time and many found the Saviour, and most of them are here to-day. But three years before that Komatsu San had come to your village, and for those three years had prayed and waited for God's time to proclaim the Gospel. Today we gather to praise God for what He has done in the past eight years. You have all done well, but Komatsu San has exceeded. Under God you owe all to her and to her sacrificial work. Now, as you know, our sister is seriously ill; indeed we did not think she would have been able to be present today, but God has strenthened her and she is with us. Soon she is going to heaven, and I want you all to give her a real clap as we send her off."

At once the church resounded with the vigorous clapping of the whole congregation and the pastor had considerable difficulty in restraining their enthusiasm. Poor Komatsu San stood there bowing frequently, her eyes filled with tears. Then she spoke, and her voice could only with difficulty be heard throughout the building. It obviously pained her to make this effort.

"Dear friends of Sawadani, it is nothing that I have done. If any blessing has been poured out here it is the work of God and all the glory is His. I did not believe it possible that God would do all this in eight years. When I asked Pastor Hashimoto to come for meetings I asked him to make for me five prayer partners. Instead God has saved a multitude of souls, and we have even been able to build this lovely church. Then Takahashi San here has been able to enter Bible School and, God willing, will graduate next year and return here as the first pastor. I am overwhelmed by what God has done. This is

His doing, and the result of the faith and patience of you all. May God bless you all!"

This little message, spoken with difficulty, raised yet another storm of clapping, during which Komatsu San resumed her seat and looked almost completely exhausted.

Pastor Nagashima took the prayer of dedication for the new building, and Pastor Hashimoto followed on with his message of dedication, taking as his text "Holiness becometh Thy House, O Lord, for ever".

Finally various influential members of the community gave short messages of greeting. Among these were the chairman of the Village Council. He had reason to know what a change the Gospel had made in the village. Only three years after the meetings had started he was able to report at the annual village meeting that the morals of the community had greatly improved. Whereas at one time there had been quite a number of illegitimate children born each year, he reported that the previous year there had been but one. He did not, of course, state this in his public greetings, but he did mention how wonderfully the young people of the village had been changed, and paid glowing tribute to their hard work and industry in building the church. In a real and good way they had put Sawadani on the map, and he extended to the Christians, on behalf of the Village Council, his warm congratulations.

The chairman of the Education Committee followed, and as a schoolteacher he emphasised how glad he was to think that such splendid ethical teaching would be available to the children and young people of their village now that the church had been built. He urged the parents to let their children attend the meetings with confidence. Others followed, and there were a few congratulatory telegrams from interested friends in other towns.

So with praise and thanksgiving the proceedings came to an end, and each one present received a little box of rice-cakes as a souvenir when they left the building.

Before he left to return to Kobe, Hashimoto Sensei went over to see Sumi San. He knew full well he might never meet her again in the flesh.

"Well, Komatsu San, how are you feeling this morning?"

"Thank you, Pastor, the Lord is sustaining me, and I was so glad to be able to be present at the dedication yesterday."

Hashimoto San looked for a moment at the swollen neck and face and the weakened body. Then he said:

"Komatsu San, you have done enough, and you have suffered a great deal. I think your work here in Sawadani is finished. God has answered your prayers, the church has been built and a fine group of Christians raised up. It is nearly time for you to return to heaven. Remember Jesus said 'In my Father's house are many resting places . . . I go to prepare a place for you!' He has a place ready for you, and soon He will welcome you there."

"Yes, Pastor, I think you are right. I am very tired, and now that the church is finished I can rest in peace. Indeed I cannot work any more. God has answered prayer abundantly, abundantly. Soon I shall just return to Heaven, and meet the Lord Jesus there."

Her voice was very low and came with great difficulty. So the pastor bowed his head and prayed, thanking God for His great work through His servant, for His grace, manifested in her life; asking Him to sustain her daily and bring her safely through the valley of the shadow of death to the heavenly uplands of light and glory. Their tears mingled with their prayers and praises as they waited before the Lord.

"Goodbye, Komatsu San. We will meet in the Morning!"

"Yes, Pastor, in the Morning. Goodbye, and thank you for all you have done!"

Chapter 18

NO TEMPLE THERE

THE dedication service over, Takahashi San returned to his studies in Kobe and Komatsu San continued to live in the little house on the hillside above Chihara with old Mrs. Nakajima to care for her. Her needs were few. Indeed she would spend no money on medicine but squeezed out the juices of herbs and grasses, which she drank to help deaden the pain. After a month or so her condition became worse. As the cancerous fibres spread into the throat it became increasingly difficult for her to breathe and her face became more swollen. The doctor was called, but he shook his head and confirmed that there was nothing that could be done. She might last another month or two, but that was all.

One day Sumi San was greatly cheered by a visit from Mr. and Mrs. Koide. Their coming seemed to bring back to her all the wonderful dealings of God with her back in the Mikage days.

"Komatsu San, it will not be long before all your pain and suffering is over and you will be at home with the Lord."

"Koide San, my suffering is small compared with what Jesus Christ suffered for me. When I think how wilful and stubborn I was, it is a wonder to me that God loved me at all. You were so patient too. I'm afraid you must often have thought me rude and ungrateful in those days; but I didn't know the love of God then."

"You have been through very sad experiences, Sumi San, but God was gradually drawing you to Himself. We didn't know then what purposes He had in store for your life. Just think of all God has done in this village. All the early experiences of your life were to fit you and prepare you for this piece of service. Is not your heart happy as you think of all that God has done?"

"Very happy, Koide San, very happy! The early experiences of my life were very bitter, and I became very hard towards God and man. But the Lord won my stubborn heart. I don't think

I could ever have had patience in the testing and persecution we have had here if I had not passed through those fiery trials myself. Truly 'He hath done all things well!'

"Yes, all things well, all things well," she reiterated. Her voice was weak and came with obvious effort.

"Sumi San, don't say any more, just rest. We will sing to you, and read and pray with you."

"Thank you." She closed her eyes with a happy smile upon her face. The two old friends prayed and sang, and read words of comfort and assurance from the Book of books, while Sumi San lay quietly in her quilts on the matted floor.

The weeks passed by and the last heat of summer disappeared with the oncoming of the fall of the year. The rice had been harvested, threshed and stored away, and the farmers were busy making preparation for the cold winter ahead, when Sumi San took a decided turn for the worse. Her days too had come to the winter of life and just before her lay the cold chill of death. For Sumi San this held no fears—she had long since made preparation, and there was a light in the valley for her.

At the beginning of December a wire reached Takahashi San at the Bible School, and he was given permission by the principal to return to Sawadani owing to Sumi San's critical condition. The long journey home completed, he made his way as soon as possible to the little cottage and entered. The old woman greeted him.

"Ah, Takahashi San, honourably return. I hope you are well."

"Yes, thank you, I am well, but how is Komatsu San?"

The old lady shook her head and said:

"You have just come in time. It cannot be long now."

"Is she conscious?"

"Oh yes, but the growth in the throat makes it impossible for her to eat much or say much. Will you come in?"

"Thank you," and he slipped out of his shoes and stepped up into the house.

Sumi San was in the inner six-mat room, lying on her quilts. At her head was her Bible and hymn-book, while in other parts of the small room were flowers brought by the Christians, the lovely chrysanthemums of the Japanese autumn. On a small chest-of-drawers was a copy of Hoffman's famous picture of Christ in Gethsemane. By turning her head slightly Sumi San could see this representation of her Master in His hour of suffering, and it comforted her.

As Takahashi San spoke, Sumi San turned toward him and smiled. Her face was emaciated and rendered misshapen by the cancerous growth, but the same confident smile was there, shining out of the clear eyes.

"Torao San, honourably return," she whispered, and lifted her left hand to greet him. He took it in his and knelt down beside the quilts.

"Komatsu San, is it very painful?"

"At times, but God gives me strength every day."

"I'm sure He does. It will not be long now before He takes you to Himself, and then all your suffering will be over."

"Yes, it won't be long now."

Both were silent for a few moments, and then Sumi San said:

"Torao San, put your hand under the *futon* here. You will feel a packet there. Please pull it out."

Takahashi San put his hand in between the quilts and the straw floor-mats and pulled out a paper packet, which he handed to her. But Sumi San refused to take it, instead letting her hand rest upon his and the packet it held as she said:

"Torao San, there is fifteen thousand yen in that."

"What is it for?"

"Torao San, next year you will graduate from Bible School and become an evangelist. An evangelist in Japan never has a great deal of money, and you will not be able to buy clothes. I saved this up and wanted to use it to buy you a suit of clothes when you graduated. I thought at that time I would live to see you graduate, but I am going to heaven. So I want you to use this to buy a suit."

It was a long speech, spoken in a whisper throughout, and Sumi San was exhausted at its completion. As for Takahashi San, his hand trembled as he held the packet and his eyes filled with tears.

"Komatsu San, how greatly you have loved me; just as a mother would her son. You help pay my expenses at Bible School, you will not spend money on medicines and drink the juice of herbs instead, and now you offer me this. Komatsu San, I cannot take this, I simply cannot! Your need is greater than mine. Please use it for yourself!"

"No, Torao San, I don't need it, for I am going to heaven.

You are going to suffer hardship as a good soldier of Jesus Christ and do the work of an evangelist. You use it—please use it!"

"Komatsu San, I cannot take it from you, really I cannot; but if you press it upon me I will hold it for a while till I know what God's will is."

Takahashi San was rather worried lest the exertion of conversation should prove too much for Sumi San.

"That's right, Torao San, you take it. Then here are my last words and my will," and she pulled an envelope out from beneath the quilt at her head. "Please give these to the Christians."

A few more days passed and the first Sunday in December came around. Takahashi San took the services in the church and special prayer was asked for Sumi San, for all knew the end was near. The following evening, Monday, a few of the Christians gathered in her little cottage and after chatting to her had a short time of praise and worship. When asked if she had a special hymn she would like sung, she chose one written by that Japanese saint of God, Tetsusaburo Sasao. The believers sang it through while Sumi San listened with eyes closed, smiling.

> *The dark night of this transient world*
> *Is passing swift away;*
> *Soon now will come the dawning bright*
> *Of that triumphal day.*
>
> *I too shall rise to heavenly heights*
> *And meet my Saviour there,*
> *I then shall see Him face to face,*
> *His glorious image share.*
>
> *The Saviour whom I long have loved*
> *A place for me did make,*
> *And there together we shall dwell*
> *When endless day shall break.*
>
> *Then hasten, O thou glorious day,*
> *Here I cannot abide.*
> *O come, my Lord, do not delay,*
> *And take me to Thy side.*

The hymn over, Sumi San opened her eyes and said a faint "Amen!" Then the believers went home, leaving just Takahashi San and his younger brother and Nitta San's daughter and one other. It was eleven o'clock, and the little group watched and waited. They knew it must be soon when He would "take her to His side".

About midnight Sumi San was in considerable pain and her breathing seemed to stop. The doctor was sent for at once. The watching friends felt sure she had passed away, but after a while she breathed again, opened her eyes and said in a whisper:

"I thought I had gone to heaven, but I'm still here. What a pity!"

There was not the slightest fear of death, and Sumi San was smiling sweetly. From then on for about thirty minutes she was quite peaceful and asked them to pray and sing. They sang her favourite hymn again and yet again. She was conscious all the time, but seemed to revive and relapse into quietude and then revive again. Then while they were singing she was gone and the extended hand grew limp and cold. Gone? Yes, from this earthly scene which had opened and closed for her in suffering. Gone? Yes, into the hill of the Lord, to dwell in His holy place, a sinner redeemed by precious blood.

Two days later the funeral service was held in the newly dedicated church and Pastor Hashimoto came up from Takasago for the occasion. Some time before the service was due to begin the church was crowded, with many people standing outside and looking in. This was the first Christian funeral in Chihara, though old Mr. Hasegawa, the carpenter, had died while the church was being built and a Christian funeral had been held in Kokonoka-ichi. This time the people who gathered were largely those who had been helped by Sumi San—the sick to whom she had ministered, the mothers whose children she had delivered, and of course the many, both young and old, who had been helped by her in spiritual things. As each came to the building they brought a small gift of money suitably wrapped in specially prepared paper. When the gifts were all counted it was found that more "flower money" had been contributed than ever before in the history of the village. There was more than sufficient to cover all the expenses of the funeral.

Inside, the church was beautifully decorated with late autumn flowers, and a simple service was conducted by the pastor. The villagers were obviously impressed by the note of reality and joy that pervaded the proceedings. There was none of the sickly-sweet smell of incense, the hollow-sounding gong, the rattling of the sistra, all of which seem but to emphasise the hopelessness of a Buddhist funeral. Here was victory—the victory of the Living Christ over death and the grave! Here was a living hope that reached past the grave to an assured eternity beyond!

Among those present was the village mayor, and at the end of the service he spoke briefly in appreciation of all that Komatsu San had done. Speaking as a non-Christian Japanese would, as though Sumi San were still there, he said:

"You were in this village only three or four years, but you have left an abiding and eternal work. You lit in this village the light of Jesus and it will burn on and on. How changed the village has become, how different now are our young people! You have indeed saved the souls of the people of this community. You died at fifty years of age, but this village will always be different because of your service. Thank you so much!"

This was indeed high praise from the head of the village where the Gospel had been so much spoken against, and where the Christians had been time and again persecuted. Faith and patience, praise and solid integrity had won the day, and back of all was the self-sacrificial life of Sumi San herself.

The problem of a burial-place for Christian believers is a serious one in the country towns and villages of Japan where Buddhism has held sway for centuries. Indeed the priest feels he must be on hand at every funeral within his parish, so that at the funeral of the Christian carpenter he had been present, complete in ceremonial robes, banging his gong while the pastor conducted the service, and nothing would dissuade him. In Sumi San's case Watanabe San had come forward and offered a portion of his own ground for a grave. Not far above his own home, at the foot of the hill, a plot of ground had been set aside as a cemetery for his own family, and here Komatsu San was laid to rest.

The service being ended, the coffin was carefully carried up the narrow pathway, along the narrow trails between the dry, stubble-covered rice-fields, and at length up the slight slope to the grave. The villagers followed in a long line reaching from the church to the elevation where the grave had been prepared. There, with a further simple service, the mortal remains of the little nurse were committed to the earth, to wait until the day dawn and the shadows flee away.

It would be impossible to think of a more suitable place. Standing at the graveside, one may look down the hillside to where the little church stands with its white cross pointing heavenwards. Then as the eye is lifted one's gaze is directed over the roofs of Chihara to the scattered homes in other parts of Sawadani, and farther still to the opening of the valley where it joins that formed by the Go River. This was the sphere of Sumi San's labour; and here it was that God had used the vessel He had fashioned, to build to His eternal glory a temple of living stones—His Church.

Chapter 19

THE AFTER-GLOW OF GLORY

IT had been a perfect autumn day, the genial sun shining down from a clear blue sky until, its journey run, it had set behind the distant hills. And now the whole western sky was filled with amber light reaching upwards to where it merged with the blue-grey of the firmament above. The tree-lined hills stood out in dark silhouette as against a golden screen; the nearer buildings and objects were etched in deep purple. It was God's after-glow, the final reminder of the glory of the day that was done; and, yet again, the assurance of a new day to follow. And then, as if a curtain had dropped and shut off the scene, it was night!

So with Komatsu San. For a while her life in Christ had been "as the sun shineth in his strength". Many had felt its genial warmth and been blessed. But now her sun had set, yet so bright had been the day that the after-glow of glory lingered on, and with it the assurance of the dawn of the new, eternal day. Then she would rise in glory!

.　　.　　.　　.　　.

Later on the evening of the funeral day some of the Christians gathered together and read Sumi San's brief and simple will. In it she stated that she wished all her goods to be given to the various Christians in Sawadani, while her younger brother was appointed to settle her final affairs.

Among her belongings was her cash-book, carefully kept down through the years and indeed right up to the end. From her early days Sumi San had been schooled in thrifty ways, and later when she had found the Saviour she learned that money is a trust from God. Thereafter every penny was carefully accounted for and handled with scrupulous care and integrity. When the Christians checked her actual cash against the entries in the cash-book they found that five yen was missing —a small, inconsequential amount. But as they continued their sorting of her belongings and were removing some goods from her chest-of-drawers, out fell a five-yen piece! Sumi San had kept her personal accounts to the last yen! It was this practical righteousness that had lent such power to her life and witness in the village. Her religion was not a mere formal thing, a matter of convenience. Her faith was vital, living, central in all the varied relationships of life, and in that it differed vastly from the heathen cults around her.

Before he returned to Bible School Takahashi San spoke to the church officials about Sumi San's last gift to him. He explained how he felt that he could not keep the money. "This is not for me. It belongs to God", and forthwith he handed them the money for their disposal. However, after prayer and discussion the officers felt that they ought to respect the wish expressed by Sumi San before she died, and they accordingly returned the most of the money to Takahashi San so that he might buy himself a suit as she had requested.

Some weeks after the funeral a simple wooden cross was erected at the grave bearing Sumi San's name and the phrase— "A Grain of Wheat". If you were to walk to the head of the grave and look at the back of the cross you would read—"In this place I wait for the new heaven and the new earth wherein dwelleth righteousness."

.   .   .   .   .

The spring following Sumi San's death Takahashi Torao San graduated from the Bible School, and as he ascended the rostrum to receive his diploma he wore the suit that the nurse's last sacrificial gift had purchased. He returned to Sawadani and there entered upon his pastoral duties, living in the simple quarters prepared for him in the church. After a year or so it was there that he welcomed his bride—Miss Nitta, and now together they live and witness for Christ there.

Nor have the Christians been idle. They have completely tiled the roof of the church at the cost of some eighty thousand yen. But where did the money come from? Again it was largely the result of the young people's efforts. Through the summer they gathered *kaya*, a kind of tough reed used in making bales for charcoal, and in the long winter months they spent many an evening singing and having fellowship together as they plied their fingers at this task. Or else they earned money by cutting and hauling wood from the mountains. Now, as before, the young people have hardly any money except at the New Year or at the time of the O Bon festival. Little by little the money was saved and now the church is resplendent with its brick-red tiles. There are still further plans to be carried into effect—for example, the provision of chairs or benches for the church—and the Christians continue to work towards this end with a will.

There have been changes in the Christian group too, for a number of the young people have married and set up homes. Ueki San had the distinction of being the first one married in the church, when he received a fine girl from Izumo as his wife. He and Otani San, also married, live right alongside the church, and the young pastor of the church is rejoicing in the gradual increase in the number of Christian homes. He knows this helps the stability of the church. Sugimoto San is still the "ruling elder" with his sane and solid advice, and while Takahashi San was in Bible School was a tremendous help in building up the Christians in their faith. There is still a measure of persecution, although the church has become an accepted fact in the village. To this day some of the children in high school are forbidden by their parents to attend the Sunday school and the services.

The good work of evangelism is progressing also. Sumi San's brother became an enquirer, and some of her relatives living near Akana have also sought the Way. Pastor Takahashi has been able to have cottage meetings in their home, and God is fulfilling His promise "thou shalt be saved and thy house". Sometimes the Christians hire a motor vehicle and go out to some other village, and gradually people living in other valleys are hearing of Christ.

"I will build My Church," affirmed the Lord Jesus Christ, and in at least this one mountain village in Japan living stones are being built into a spiritual house acceptable to God through Him. Soon will come the day of reckoning when every man's work is tested of what sort it is. Surely then the work of the little nurse of Sawadani will be revealed as gold, silver and precious stones to the eternal praise and glory of her Master.